EVER CLOSER UNION

HUGH THOMAS'S career reflects a lifelong interest in European culture. He made his name as a historian with *The Spanish Civil War* (1961). That book was banned by General Franco's regime but it was translated into most European languages. When it was eventually published in Spain, after Franco's death, it was described by a Catalan newspaper as 'a bible for a generation of Spanish democrats in catacombs'.

His history of Cuba (*Cuba or the Pursuit of Liberty*, 1971) has played a similar part in the life of Cuban exiles. His *Armed Truce* (1987) analysed the causes, and the early months, of the Cold War, above all in Eastern Europe; and *The Unfinished History of the World* (1979) sought to place the history of Europe in its global context.

The Spanish Civil War won the Somerset Maugham Prize in 1962, and *The Unfinished History of the World* the Arts Council Prize for History in 1980.

An earlier attempt of his to persuade British opinion to take full advantage of the European Community was *Europe, the Radical Challenge*, 1973. He is at present working on a history of the Conquest of Mexico.

Hugh Thomas became a life peer in 1981 and often speaks on European issues in the House of Lords.

This essay is dedicated
to those of my friends
who disagree with its conclusion.

EVER CLOSER UNION
Britain's Destiny in Europe

Hugh Thomas

HUTCHINSON
LONDON SYDNEY AUCKLAND JOHANNESBURG

© Hugh Thomas 1991

The right of Hugh Thomas to be
identified as Author of this work has been asserted
by Hugh Thomas in accordance with the
Copyright, Designs and Patents Act, 1988

All rights reserved

This edition first published in 1991 by
Hutchinson

An early version of this essay was delivered as The
Martin Wight memorial lecture at The University of
Sussex, 8 May 1990, and appeared in *The World
Today*, August/September 1990.

Random Century Group Ltd
20 Vauxhall Bridge Road, London SW1V 2SA

Random Century Australia (Pty) Ltd
20 Alfred Street, Milsons Point, Sydney, NSW 2061, Australia

Random Century New Zealand Ltd
PO Box 40–086, Glenfield, Auckland 10, New Zealand

Random Century South Africa (Pty) Ltd
PO Box 337, Bergvlei, 2012, South Africa

British Library Cataloguing in Publication Data

Thomas, Hugh *1931–*
 Ever closer union.
 1. Great Britain. Foreign relations with Western Europe.
 2. Western Europe. Foreign relations with Great Britain.
 I. Title
 327.094

ISBN 0–09–174908–5

Photoset by Speedset Ltd, Ellesmere Port
Printed and bound in Great Britain by Biddles

Contents

		Page
I	The Choices	1
II	The Implicit Commitments	12
III	What is Entailed	28
IV	Possible Policies: Withdrawal or 'Self-peripheralisation'	31
V	The Need to Devise a Frame: Sovereignty, Union, Federation, Confederation	46
VI	Subsidiarity	55
VII	European Democracy	61
VIII	European Defence	66
IX	European Money	72
X	The Community and the Rest of Europe	82
XI	And the Consequences are . . .	90

It requires experience in government to know the immense distance between planning and executing. All the difficulty is with the last. It requires no small labour to open the eyes of either the public or of individuals, but when that is accomplished, you are not got a third of the way. The real difficulty remains in getting people to apply the principles which they have admitted, and of which they are now so fully convinced. Then springs the mine of private interests and personal animosity . . .

Lord Shelburne, c. 1800

I
The Choices

Britain faces a choice. We must choose between joining actively in a series of European political and economic experiments, knowing that they may end by causing us to become part of something which will be certainly more than a European confederation, as that word is normally used; or, we must choose to remain outside, either fully or partially, in an isolation which could turn out to be inglorious or even ruinous. The two conferences which began in Rome at the end of 1990 about, respectively, economic and monetary union, and political union, may prove in retrospect to be turning points.

For both choices, the nation itself still seems, 29 years after Britain's first application to join the Community in 1961, as 'magnificently unprepared' as Rupert Brooke was said to have been for life itself. Yet there are no other possibilities. Europe for many in Britain is an unwelcome guest who, however, cannot be indefinitely put off. The changes proposed by both conferences will be presumably decided on by the end of 1991. Then, probably, they will be ratified by national Parliaments during 1992, and come into force on 1 January 1993.

The curious thing about this is that it is no longer clearly an issue of party. Anyone reading, say, the report of the debate about the future of the European Community in the House of Commons on 15 June 1990 would have been hard put to it, had he been a stranger to Britain, and if the names of those who spoke meant nothing to him, to know to what party they belonged. A Labour member of Parliament (Brian Sedgemore) was reported as saying that 'the idea of national economies controlled by national governments is dead'. A Conservative member (Nigel Forman) insisted that, in future, there would be a European federal bank. A fortnight later, on 28 June 1990, the Prime Minister, no less, suggested that she agreed, to some extent, on the matter of 'economic monetary and political union', with Tony Benn. The front benches of both parties in the House of Commons quarrel in public over Europe, as over most things. That is an institutional necessity. In practice, the front bench of the Labour party seems in 'general agreement with the Prime Minister', as a Labour spokesman in the House of Lords privately commented to me recently. The Labour party, it is true, has made substantial changes towards a European policy: for example, their support of the proposed Social Charter, or their advocacy of a continental-style railway system. But even a polemical anti-Conservative would not insist that the present Government has *no* European policy. These things did not prevent the House of Commons last year from being overwhelmingly hostile to the report on economic and monetary union prepared by Monsieur Jacques Delors and his committee.

Despite such relative, if verbal, convergence of view between the parties, there is no chance whatever of a national coalition on the European issue. Most of our political leaders may be instinctively hostile to further European integration. But they are already, as it were, embarked upon a great river. They grasp for a branch above them, or they make for the bank. But the current is remorseless. The boat carries on. Once or twice, in 1989 and 1990, the observer has had the sensation, as Keynes had at the

Paris peace conference in 1919, of 'events marching on to their fated conclusion uninfluenced and unaffected by the cerebrations of Statesmen in Council'.

The paradox is that the only party to rejoice wholeheartedly at the direction of this current are the Liberal Democrats. Yet that party is very far from power. Most people have even forgotten its new name. This is a state of affairs which will please only the minority for whom irony is the only predictable thing in politics; or, those for whom political parties are irrelevancies in the struggle for principle.

Long-term friends of British full membership of the European club may say that there is, in fact, nothing new about the present state of affairs, since the decision to participate in the European experiments was taken either in 1975, at the time of the referendum on Europe insisted upon by the Labour Government of Harold Wilson; or in 1972 at the time of the European Communities Act, which was passed by Edward Heath's Government. They might alternatively say that the decisive occasion, as insisted upon by Douglas Hurd, in an eloquent chapter in his book *An End of Promises*, was the vote in the House of Commons on 28 October 1971, after five days of debate. Yet Harold Macmillan thought the 'turning point in our history' to have been 27 July 1961, when the British cabinet (including Enoch Powell, then Minister of Health) agreed that the Government should make a formal application to accede to the Treaty of Rome. A good case can be made for any of those 'historic' occasions as 'turning points' in Britain's relations with the Community.

Yet, to paraphrase A.J.P. Taylor, they were turning points in British history about which British history failed to turn. For, perhaps through the neglect of those friends of full membership of the European club (of whom I have been one), the questions have come in 1990 to be newly posed. Politics, as well as history, repeats itself.

Politicians also repeat one another. Students of the controversy on European monetary union, now under way, should recall the speech on the matter by James Callaghan, on 28 October 1971, in the European debate in the House of Commons to which I referred earlier; or, if you believe that Europe should never be more than a *Europe des patries*, you could do worse than to look even further back, at the exchange of letters between Harold Macmillan and Jean Monnet at the Council of Europe in 1950. Macmillan opposed the plan to set up a Coal and Steel Community by the suggestion that the proposed High Authority should consist of a 'committee of representatives from the coal and steel industries of the different countries'. Monnet replied: 'co-operation between nations, while essential, cannot alone meet our problem. What must be sought is a fusion of interests of the European peoples, not merely an effort to maintain an equilibrium of these interests through additional machinery for negotiation.' The phraseology has a modern ring.

Others who believe that they are saying something original in 1990 may not like to be reminded that the Foreign Secretary in 1961 (Lord Home) said: 'Let me admit at once that the Treaty of Rome would involve a considerable derogation of sovereignty.' Others still could do worse than to recall Tony Benn's letter to his constituents in Bristol, at the time of the referendum in 1975: 'Britain's continuing membership of the Community would mean the end of Britain as a completely self-governing nation.'

In 1990, many 'senior Conservatives' were often heard to say that they did not want their party divided over Europe as it had been over Ireland in the days of Peel. Yet Macmillan confided the same reflection to his diary in May 1961: 'there are many very *anxious* Conservatives. It is getting terribly like 1846.' (Referring to his colleagues, he nevertheless added: 'anyway none of these can be Disraeli to my Peel.') These references may seem increasingly appropriate now that Europe is taking on, for twentieth-century Britain, some of the elements which marked Ireland in the nineteenth: a never-ending argument.

THE CHOICES

Any investigation of the reason for this new posing of old questions necessitates, to some extent, an examination of the substance of the issue. On the one hand, it did not seem, in the late 1970s or early 1980s, even to pro-Europeans, that the long-term destiny of Europe would be discussed for a long time, if ever. The price of 'sheep-meat', as mutton and lamb are, inelegantly if Europeanly known, had, for example, to be resolved first. 'Not in my lifetime' was a much-used phrase on the lips of British statesmen, who believed that the next stage of European integration, if there were to be one, could, and should, be postponed till the Greek Kalends. The ambitions of the 'founding fathers' of the Community seemed to have been banished forever by General de Gaulle. The Utopian days at Strasbourg in the late 1940s seemed faraway memories, forming short chapters in autobiographies whose authors, soon after, turned to high politics, such as Soviet and Middle East affairs. The campaign in Britain to join the Community lasted a long time – from 1961, when Harold Macmillan at last uncoiled himself from his studied langour to submit our first application for membership, until 1975, when the vote was counted in the only nationwide referendum which Britain has experienced. Indeed, the political battle had lasted so long that the combatants, the victors included, were exhausted. Since, *mirabile dictu*, Britain was within the walls of Europe, the nation, the victors perhaps assumed, would probably accept everything which followed, without demur. It might not even notice further integration, should it occur. They European Movement shrivelled, while its leading members left for Brussels to work in the Commission. Edward Heath merely glowered. 'Europeans', who were also 'free marketeers', neglected Europe, as indeed did I, while speaking of the need for the revival of capitalism, even if that seemed, at the time, to be 'capitalism in one country'.

The neglect since 1975 by the 'Europeans' among us to address ourselves to the large issue at stake about the destiny of

Europe was a mistake. We should have insisted, forcefully and loudly, that we had agreed, by the terms of the preamble to the Treaty of Rome, to associate ourselves with an organisation whose long-term aim was explicitly to achieve 'an ever closer union' of the European peoples. We should have discussed what that grand phrase, 'ever closer union', meant. We had accepted, after all, the *acquis communautaire*, the accumulated wisdom and aspirations of the six founding nations, before we joined. We should have drawn attention to the commitment of 1969 to pursue economic and monetary union. Nor should we have forgotten that one-third of our population who had voted against membership of the Community in the referendum. We should have directed ourselves subtly to them, and to their fears that, in agreeing to 'join Europe' something, perhaps much, might be lost of that essential 'Englishness' – 'Britishness', if you insist – which has given our insular yet global nation its singularity. Our old national identity as a 'thalassocracy', or as a great sea monster which, in Heine's image, could always crawl back to its island cave when wounded in the seas off the Continent, still, it seems, means much to them; even if the island cave is now less easily protected. To such people it is no use, even now, saying that much of traditional Britain has already been lost. Yet it has. Recall, for example, George Eliot's *Adam Bede* where the hero, a carpenter, reflects: 'It's fine talking about having supper when there's a coffin promised to be ready at Brox'on by seven o'clock tomorrow morning and ought to ha' been there now and not a nail struck yet.' That is to be reminded of an era when hard work and punctual deliveries were normal in England. Nothing indicates more the change which has come to Britain in the last 40 years than a sentence in Geoffrey Grigson's *The English Character* (1955): '. . . this orderliness and gentleness, this absence of overt aggression, calls for an explanation if the dynamics of the English character are to be effectively described.' The loyalties of traditionalists were not faced by the 'Europeans' among us because, in the years after 1975, they, we, were engaged in Britain in what seemed a more immediate issue, a positively Gaullist task; the business of national recovery. The 1970s were the years when Lord Goodman was heard remarking: 'This country is on a knife's edge. It could go either way'; and when Lord Hailsham believed that Britain had reached the City of Destruction, but one in which there was no wicket gate.

The great events of the late 1970s and 1980s were distinctly non-European. First, there was the appearance of Margaret Thatcher's philosophy of the free market as a new, and unprecedented, brand of British conservatism; and second, there was the emergence of the Social Democrats. The new Conservatives were primarily preoccupied by the national question. So too, in general, were the Social Democrats, even if their leaders were 'Europeans'. Both shared, to varying degrees, a vision of Britain sinking into a slough of despond as a preliminary, or so it seemed, to becoming a Soviet dependency. We had surely to save ourselves, naturally, before we could devote attention to our new stall in the main street of the European Community. The chief external problem of those days seemed to be the Soviet threat – which, knowing what we know now of Soviet economic weakness, we may have exaggerated;* and the main domestic one, the business of regeneration of British society and economy – the difficulty of which no doubt we underestimated.

So far as Europe was concerned, Mrs Thatcher's first administration turned its attention, successfully, to such questions as the British contribution to the European budget, an important matter of principle. Her second Government interested itself in the need to reform the common agricultural policy – a Herculean task and one as yet incomplete. In her third term, her ministers set out to secure the completion of the Single

*It can, however, be represented that the Soviet threat under Brezhnev was at its most dangerous, and so it is wrong to suggest that it was overestimated. Economically weak powers with large military machines are always menacing.

Market by the year 1992, with the full enactment of the famous 282 measures demanded in the Community's white paper. That last task was, or at least seemed to be, an affair of ideology: capitalist ideology. We thought then that, to ensure that the Common Market worked properly for all the 320-million 'European Community Nationals' (as we are now all called – even at British airports), and to guarantee that the non-tariff restrictions on trade came to an end, would be worthy enough achievements for the 1990s. Article 13 of the Single European Act provided, in no uncertain terms, for an 'internal market [after 1992] ... without internal frontiers, in which the free movement of goods, persons, services and capital is ensured'; a colossal change, if achieved. The stage after that, if there were to be one, would, we assumed, be a matter for the next generation. In addition, despite the arguments about other matters, Britain could boast that she had done more to prepare the way for the single market than the other members. Her claim to have enacted directives of the community more promptly than other nations was valid too, as the Summit at Dublin (April 1990) graciously recognised. Her complaints at the non-fulfilments of some other nations (such as Italy) are also quite justified.

There did not seem then, in, say, 1985, any long-term issue at hand; any doubts felt by the good European about Mrs Thatcher's Governments' attitudes towards the Community were laid to rest by the Prime Minister's signature of the Solemn Declaration of Stuttgart in 1983; and even more by the passage through Parliament of the Bill ratifying the Single European Act of 1987 (by use of the guillotine), with its, by implication, radical innovation: the introduction of qualified majority voting (Article 7 of the Act). (This, incidentally, revised the promise, in the white paper of 1971 commending accession, that 'On a question where a Government considers that vital national interests are involved, it is established that a decision should be unanimous'.) Meantime, the Labour party remained divided about the European

Community. It was difficult, in the 1970s and 1980s, to see even a wisp of the smoke of new thought emanating from their factory chimneys on that subject. (The exception was the small group of intellectuals surrounding *The Left Review* who were influenced by Italian Communists to support the idea of a United *Socialist* States of Europe.)

The Conservatives were thus entitled, in the election of 1987, to claim to be 'the party of Europe' and to say, in their electoral manifesto of that year, that they had 'taken Britain from the sidelines into the mainstream of Europe'; a metaphor no less effective for being mixed. The party's manifesto for the European elections of 1989 did, it is true, have a *caveat*: it was 'not only unrealistic, but damaging' to speculate on long-term issues until the single market had been achieved. That argument might have been disappointing to an orthodox visionary who always, like Wilde, wishes to have Utopia somewhere on his map. But the phrase would have seemed appropriate, even in 1987, to the 'founding fathers' of the new Europe, had they still been alive. They had known that the states of Europe would not want to sign away their independence at a great international conference in, say, the Galerie des Glaces at Versailles, even if they would be happy to tie the shoe-laces of integration wherever they could: *Suaviter in modo; fortiter in re.*

The British subscription to that last approach was well summed up in an exchange between Lord Ardwick, a Labour peer and ex-editor, and Malcolm Rifkind, then Minister of State at the Foreign Office, at a hearing of the Select Committee of the House of Lords in 1985. Lord Ardwick said: 'One of the problems between continental member states and ourselves is that most of them believe it is essential to define a goal, because the definition impels progress to that goal ... we prefer to go along and get there in the long run without defining the ideal.' Malcolm Rifkind replied: 'We would take the view, if you tried to identify on tablets of stone exactly what the final objective is, then you will spend an enormous amount of time discussing it and you will be unlikely to agree. If you concentrated on what are the measures that will make sense and will be helpful and useful, their achievement will be a very important and vital contribution to European Union.'

Few people in Britain in the 1980s, therefore, thought much about the long-term future of Europe, or considered it necessary to do so. Even energetic Europeans assumed that the chances of achieving much in the way of a political union had been ruined by General de Gaulle, whose shadow seemed forever to lie over France. In Britain 'Europe' was handled by the Foreign Office whose prudent habit as a department had been, for several generations, to eschew thinking about the distant future. 'The British as a nation have never been good at long-term planning', wrote Sir William Hayter, one of Britain's best ambassadors to Moscow, in 1960, 'they live from day to day, deciding questions as they come up sensibly enough, but never foreseeing what questions will come up, or considering where they ultimately want to go. The Foreign Office is very like this.' 'Concepts' or 'grand designs', were best left to Henry Kissinger. What was true of the 1950s was equally true of the 1980s. In 1980, I recall handing to an official a copy of that famous paper of 1950 NSC68, which indicated cogently, at length, what attitude the United States should have to Stalin's expansionism. His reaction was: 'We could produce nothing like that nowadays.'

This institutional reluctance to look far ahead has been the case as much as ever when the matter concerned has been, as 'Europe' has been, less a matter of international policy, in the old style, than of formulating a much more complicated plan for something occupying the mezzanine floor between foreign and domestic interests. The Foreign Office would have been distressed had someone proposed a Royal Commission to devise a long-term plan for Britain in a Europe committed to integration, rather as Lord Durham devised a plan in 1840 for

THE CHOICES

'holding on to the colonies by letting them go', in order to become Dominions. But there is no evidence that they prepared such a plan themselves. If they did, there was no communication with the public, in the form of a white paper describing what the policy was.

An anecdote will illustrate the point which I am making, better than anything. In 1976, I lunched with James Callaghan (then Foreign Secretary) to welcome Señor José Maria Areilza, the first Spanish Foreign Minister to visit England since the accession of King Juan Carlos the previous autumn. Both Foreign Secretaries mentioned European Union in their speeches. My neighbour, a Spanish official, turned to me and asked: 'What actually do the British understand by that expression?' I turned to my other neighbour, a political adviser to James Callaghan, and said that I thought that he should answer the question. He took a deep breath and said: 'Well, Harold Wilson [he was still Prime Minister] has always said that British foreign policy is like an old stagecoach. It goes slowly and no one knows where it is going. But it always gets to its destination in the end.' My Spanish friend remarked: 'I understand that is your approach. But, you know, we Latins like to know where we are going on a journey before we start off.'

II

The Implicit Commitments

In the 1990s the ambitions of the founders of the European Community – Jean Monnet, Robert Schuman, Alcide de Gasperi and Konrad Adenauer – look like, after all, coming to something. The ritual toasts to their memories at grand occasions of the Community have suddenly seemed to be glasses held up to statesmen more substantial than ghosts.

British politicians always knew of those men's ambitions, or should have done. The hope of organising, or the need to organise, Europe on 'a federal basis' was mentioned in the very first French declaration of 1950 proposing a Coal and Steel Community. That document continued: 'A Franco-German union is an essential element in it, and the French Government has decided to act to this end ... even if obstacles accumulated from the past make it impossible to achieve immediately the close association which the French Government has as its aim.' That was, in one sense, the European Community's founding statement.

Similar goals were written into the preambles of the Coal and Steel Community in 1950, and of the Treaty of Rome in 1957. It was because Britain had doubts about the consequent implications – 'obstacles from the past' – that the Labour Government in 1950 refused to take part in the discussions leading to the Coal and Steel Community. They did so in terms not unlike those used by British officials about the idea of economic amd monetary union in 1990: 'After the most careful study of the French memorandum, it remains the view of His Majesty's Government that to subscribe to the terms of the draft communiqué . . . would involve entering into an advance commitment to pool coal and steel resources and to set up an authority, with certain supreme powers, before there had been a full opportunity to consider how these powers would work in practice.'

Alan Bullock, in his biography of the then Foreign Secretary, Ernest Bevin, gave the background to that decision. Bevin was close to death, and 'was taking sedative drugs which made him doze off quite soundly during . . . discussion'. The British Government was also angry not to have been consulted by the French before the latter made their initial suggestion. At the critical moment, the Prime Minister, Clement Attlee, and the Chancellor of the Exchequer, Sir Stafford Cripps, were away on holiday. The acting Prime Minister, Herbert Morrison, went to the theatre. Tracked down later at the Ivy Restaurant, the famous theatrical establishment off Shaftesbury Avenue, he told the Minister of State at the Foreign Office, Kenneth Younger, and a senior official, Sir Edwin Plowden, who accompanied him: 'It's no good. We can't do it. The Durham miners won't wear it.' A plaque might be added to the walls of The Ivy to commemorate that, at that time, typically English remark. Sir Henry Irving at least would have appreciated it.

There was little division about Europe between the British parties in those early days. The founder of the European Movement, Churchill, was ambiguous about Britain's role in Europe. In his famous speech at Zürich (1945), he encouraged the French and the Germans to create a United States of Europe. He thought the British should be outside; godfathers to the idea, not practitioners. Churchill saw Britain as the nerve centre of a still potentially powerful Commonwealth, and as banker to the sterling area. The idea of close political association, or of federation with the countries of the Continent, seemed wrong to him, especially when, a generation before, the country had never seriously considered the (at first sight more appealing) idea of an imperial federation, put forward by Joseph Chamberlain. Hence the series of hesitations which characterised British policy towards Europe between 1946 and 1961 – the recollection of which offers some odd morals to those who have heard the same symphony repeated in a different scale, with different orchestration, and new players, in the 1980s.

Reading of the postwar era in British politics towards Europe, it is difficult to avoid the impression that it was a time when a number of great men, widely considered, man for man, somewhat superior to the present generation of politicians, had no clear idea what they were doing. Thus there were many meetings about securing 'closer union' with Europe, toasts to 'United Europe', even suggestions for a European cabinet. But when Churchill said at Strasbourg that he supported European union, but was against federalism, it is hard today to see what he meant. In 1950 he called for the 'immediate creation of a unified European army' and for a 'European Minister of Defence'. But four years later he was dismissive of the idea of the army as a 'sludgy amalgam'. In these changes and hesitations, Churchill very well expressed the ambivalent feelings of Britain herself: then and since. In Martin Gilbert's admirable life of Churchill, there is the following characteristic sentence: 'The Cabinet concluded, however, that, if the proposal for closer association between Western Europe and the sterling area and Commonwealth came up for discussion, at the forthcoming Committee of Ministers of the Council of Europe, Britain's representative, Eden, should, after pointing out the "difficulties" of the proposal, "seek to ensure that its further discussion should be adjourned for as long as possible".'

Harold Macmillan, Prime Minister in the late 1950s, of

course knew, when in the end he submitted Britain's application to join the Community, that the founders of that body had had the design to create a United States of Europe. He was well-informed about Europe, having been Churchill's deputy at the Council of Europe in the late 1940s. Sometimes, indeed, Macmillan recognised the existence of this near federalism in public, or, at any rate, among his colleagues. Thus, in his memoirs, he tells us that the British cabinet, at their meeting on 27 July 1961, decided that 'it was in the interest of the Western world as a whole to create a truly united Europe'. 'Truly united'? Surely those words suggest the acceptance of a political union? Macmillan told the Commonwealth Prime Ministers on 10 September 1962 that 'the Governments of the Six are anxious to move forward from an economic to some form of political union for Europe'. But, he added, 'it seems clear that the approach of the six existing members of the Community is gradual and pragmatic. There is no grandiose supra-national or federalistic plan'. There was, indeed, no plan; yet there was, for most of the leaders on the Continent, except for General de Gaulle, an intention.

Macmillan knew that, presumably, but he must also have known, as Monnet had known, that the British – or, anyway, the House of Commons – would be unlikely to commit themselves to a plan involving any hint of federalism. Maurice Macmillan wrote to his father the day before the latter, as Prime Minister, made his first speech commending the Community to the Commons: 'I think that the House is, unfortunately, no more capable collectively of rational thought than the country.' Hence, Harold Macmillan – on that occasion – reassured his listeners, giving the impression even that he scarcely knew the vocabulary of the debate: there was no 'federationistic'(!) or 'federalistic' plan on the agenda. How could there be, with General de Gaulle as President of France? Like de Gaulle, the British wanted a 'Europe of states'.

This was no doubt the only way to persuade Britain to try to join the Community. The method may sound Machiavellian; an echo, perhaps, of Stanley Baldwin's determination in 1935 to underplay the extent of the German danger in order to win the election of that year – and so begin to rearm:

> In deeds of such uncertain double vision
> Safety lies only in obscurity.
> Those measures are the worst that stand avow'd;
> What's not abandoned is not wholly lost.

Macmillan was convinced that Britain's future lay in the Community, even though it was unclear what it would turn out to be. He believed that it was his responsibility to carry the country into it. His tragedy was that, though de Gaulle wanted a Europe without concessions to federalism – that is, the very Europe which the British body politic might accept – he wanted it without Britain: *'L'Europe à l'anglaise sans Angleterre.'*

By the 1960s, it did not seem that the federal plans of the Community's founders were going to prosper. De Gaulle sought the revival of France, not the unity of Europe. He said, after his retirement, to André Malraux, at Colombey-les-Deux-Églises: *'L'Europe, vous le savez comme moi, sera un accord entre les Etats ou rien.'* In a press conference in May 1962, he had said the same: 'Only states are valid, legitimate and capable of achieving [Europe] . . . at present there is no Europe other than a Europe of states – except, of course, for myths, fictions and pageants.' (Five of his ministers who favoured federalism then resigned.) The Gaullist mood was dominant not only when Britain sought first to join the Community in 1961–3, but even when she did join it in 1973 – though the General was dead. No one in France even then wished, or cared, to challenge the Gaullist legacy on that matter, even if President Pompidou relaxed so far as to permit British entry to the Community as part of the expansion of 1972–3. The first meeting of Heads of Government of the Six

THE IMPLICIT COMMITMENTS

after the death of de Gaulle, at The Hague in December 1969, spoke of the participants' 'common conviction that a Europe composed of states ... united in their essential interests ... is indispensable'.

Britain applied to join the Community a second time in 1967. Harold Wilson had convinced himself that the policy which he had questioned when it was put forward by his predecessor was by then the right one. Once again, General de Gaulle vetoed the application. He argued that Britain was still not ready – 'ripe' (*'mûre'*) – for 'life in common with the Continent'. Wilson made yet another application in 1970. An election intervened. Edward Heath carried through the application, despite a Labour change of mind. Britain eventually signed, in 1972, the Treaty of Rome – primarily for economic reasons. The main argument of those who supported that course was that the country would prosper by being part of a large market. 'Economy of scale' was the phrase on every lip. The Government felt it best to be on the inside in respect of economic policies which would obviously affect us one way or the other.

Some in those days said that they supported joining the Community 'for political reasons'. What that meant was that an association of rich countries would help to keep Western Europe out of the hands of Russia. The argument also implied, as Harold Wilson put it, when Prime Minister in 1967, that 'together we can ensure that Europe plays in world affairs the part which this Europe of today is not playing'. How that was to be assured without political union was unclear. (It was also unclear later on.) Talk of political union during the campaign over the referendum in 1975 was muted. One of Edward Heath's ministers has assured me that: 'Ted told us it was a purely commercial union. That's how we went out and sold it.' Professor Elie Kedourie, the voice of austere conservatism, has also said that that was how he saw the issue of Europe at that time. Those who stressed the political possibilities were those who opposed it: Enoch Powell,

Tony Benn, and Peter Shore. (All three were members of cabinets in 1961, or in 1967–70, which had applied to join the Community; they had not resigned, which suggests that their hostility was a kind of *l'esprit d'escalier*.) The white paper of 1971, commending an accession to the Treaty of Rome, talked about a Europe 'composed of states' as spoken of in the Communiqué of the Heads of Government of 1969; and it insisted that, 'The Community is no federation of provinces or counties. It constitutes a Community of great and established nations'. It added that the commitment to join the Community represented 'the voluntary undertaking of a sovereign state to observe policies which it has helped to form. There is no question of any erosion of essential national sovereignty; what is proposed is a sharing and an enlargement of individual national sovereignties, in the general interest'.

Admittedly, that white paper also did recall that, among the basic objectives of the Community, there figured both 'an ever closer union' and an approximation of 'economic activities'. In 1969 the Prime Ministers of the Community (of the Six) had committed themselves to achieving Economic and Monetary Union; and the Werner Report of 1970 had envisaged both a single currency and the transfer of some responsibilities for monetary and credit policy to the Community. In consequence, the 'Snake' was introduced. But that scheme met little success, largely because of the collapse of the Bretton Woods monetary system in 1973. It was true, too, that the Declaration of the first 'Summit Conference' of Heads of State and Government – the first meeting of what is now known as 'the European Council' – stated that those statesmen had 'assigned themselves the key objective of converting, before the end of this decade . . . *all* [my italics] the relationships between Member States into a European Union'. But the end of the decade came and, due to the economic crisis, went, without further changes.

Britain obviously tended to overlook that the Community had, from the beginning, been conceived as a continuing process, moving towards ever increasing integration, wherever possible. Integration was, after all, a kind of fluid which, when once squeezed into the veins of the states members, would expand. It was, for that reason, a word disliked by General de Gaulle. The report of Leo Tindemans, Prime Minister of Belgium, of 1975, ensured too that, despite the failure of the 'Snake', economic and monetary union, though never given much emphasis, should not be allowed to leave the agenda. This era of Euro-doldrums did, in the end, produce the European Monetary System (1979), even if James Callaghan's Government did not join the Exchange Rate Mechanism within it.

Yet while we assumed that we need not think about the long term, and squabbled 'pragmatically', even happily, between 1975 and 1986, about cod and pasteurised milk, the continental partners were again beginning to think differently. No doubt we should have realised, as a nation, that, for those partners, those sentences about 'ever increasing union' in the preambles of the treaties which we had signed signified something more than rhetoric. The passage by the European Parliament in 1984 of a draft treaty establishing a European Union should also have been a warning – even though, in the end, only a modified version of it would inspire the Single Act of 1987.

President Mitterrand, in particular, set about dismantling not only the communist threat in France, but also the nationalistic legacy of de Gaulle. That dismantlement will perhaps seem in history to be Mitterrand's most notable achievement; greater than his outmanoeuvring of the Communist party, which, in the age of Gorbachev, would probably have faded anyway. France had been the chief obstacle to achieving European union in the 1960s and 1970s. President Mitterrand, Europe's last great literary statesman, was a minister (even if *d'outre-mer*) in the French Government of 1950 which launched the Coal and Steel Community. He was, his brilliant biographer Catherine Nay, says, in the early 1950s 'a great partisan of Europe in general', even if a critic of the project for a European army which divided the French body politic between 1953 and 1955.

Mitterrand had challenged de Gaulle over his European policy in the presidential election of 1965. Under his management as President after 1981, France first tried, then abandoned, doctrinaire socialism, and next altered her European course. In 1983, she moved towards economic liberalism and, after a change in the value of the franc in March 1983, towards a European policy. There was, therefore, nothing to prevent the issue of both monetary and political union from being seriously raised again. The essence of Mitterrand's European reflections was that France had become too small for the fulfilment of its *mission civilisatrice*. That had to be taken over by Europe. In 1990, France, it is true, also saw European union (and monetary union, as the best way to it) as the obvious way to control, or absorb, a united Germany (and perhaps as a way of enabling her to participate in a new, economic, *Drang nach Osten*). Hence the new impatience of President Mitterrand and his Foreign Minister, Roland Dumas. All the same, the German question has only given extra urgency to plans which already existed.

How so proud, so patriotic, so self-reliant a nation as France will take to prolonged, indeed final, association with other countries must be a matter of speculation – particularly when German unity threatens the central position in Europe which France assumed would be hers. President Mitterrand will surely strive to take France back to the role of universal exemplar. France, unlike Britain and unlike the United States, has never felt doubt about its civilisation. Hence the remarkable celebration in 1989 of the Revolution. All the same, Mitterrand is taking risks. Or perhaps the dogma of *La Patrie* is so strong that it can survive any transformation, any undoing of Michelet's legacy, as well as de Gaulle's, since both would have understood the notion of an exemplary mission; indeed, de Gaulle's travels in East

Europe and his idea of a Europe from the Atlantic to the Urals, were foretastes of it.

As for Germany, support for European union was enshrined by Dr Adenauer in the Basic Law of the Federal Republic. It was also listed among the aims of the Christian Democratic Union in that party's Constitution. Dr Adenauer, the founder of both the Republic and of the party, was, after all, a Rhinelander with a contempt for the Germans of the east, especially the Protestant Prussian aristocracy. He always looked west, as Frederick the Great had done too, to France. He once said: 'A Federal Chancellor must be at once a good German and a good European.' Franz Josef Strauss said the same: 'Whoever wishes to be a German must see to it that he becomes a European while there is time.' On another occasion, Adenauer even proposed a complete union of France and Germany on the model of that suggested by Churchill to France in 1940.

European unity has always been seen, too, by Germans since 1945 as a way to obtain political influence without a rebirth of nationalism. Many times in the 1980s, furthermore, democratic Germans would be heard insisting that, unless integration in Western Europe were achieved, Western Germany would, one day, be tempted by a seductive offer of unity with East Germany on the basis of neutrality made by a Soviet Union anxious to divide the West. In particular, British neglect of the European issue, Germans would insist, pointed the way to such a new 'Rapallo'. A more positive approach was encapsulated by a slogan of Germans in all political parties: 'we should not change borders, but change what borders mean.'

The German willingness, even desire, to bury memories of the past in a European union became more relevant still when the dazzling prospect of German unity without conditions, or, at least, on West Germany's terms, suddenly appeared in 1989. As well as being a triumph for the West, this event also, of course, awoke, among some, sleeping anxieties.

Germany's continued enthusiasm for a united Europe in these new circumstances seemed to some survivors of the generation of the war to betoken a revival of hidden ambitions. Would not the new united Germany, the strongest power in the new Europe, be able to achieve by peaceful economic means what they had failed to achieve by blood and iron? But it would be to misjudge the history of Germany since 1945 to ignore that a desire to atone for acts carried out before that date has continuously motivated democratic Germany. Germany has changed. Ralf Dahrendorf years ago pointed out that the Nazis, among their destructive actions, had wholly ruined the old class system; and it seems too that the German family has been transformed from the old hierarchical autocratic structure into a far more liberal thing. The defeat of 1945 was altogether more final, because accepted as such, than that of 1918. Democratic Germany cannot be expected forever to ignore the desire of a new generation of Germans to play a part in events. Yet Chancellor Kohl was only 15 when the war was lost, his Foreign Minister, Dietrich Genscher, was 19 (though he served in the war), while their socialist opponent, Oskar Lafontaine, was less than two years old. Germans themselves have been recently free with a fine phrase of Thomas Mann's in which that novelist, in a lecture in Hamburg in 1953, advocated 'a European Germany, not a German Europe'. Recollection of that tone seems much more appropriate now than, say, what was implicit in the young Michel Debré's attack on the plan for a Coal and Steel Community nearly 40 years ago: 'You must remember that nation's lust for power, its lack of respect for freedom, its political unreliability, and, I would add, its total failure to learn the lessons of the past ... In the interests of Germany itself, Europe must not become a German Europe.' No one would deny the validity of the last phrase. But to believe that some nations are permanently condemned to evil practices is to deny several fundamental Christian and, indeed, liberal, principles; it is to come close to acceptance of a philosophy of race. West Germans, in their system of *Länder*, have worked out a good system of federal government, much superior to that of 1919–33, as, of course, of that of 1933–45. Finally, German nationalism between 1815 and 1945 was dangerous to Germany's neighbours, above all because it was a linguistic as well as a 'racial' idea. Anyone of German race and language was held, by romantics, nationalists, and Nazis, to owe allegiance to a German Fatherland. Such ideas are now far-fetched; irrelevant too, since the *volksdeutsche* population has so much diminished as a result of events between 1945 and 1947. A nation which has several million Turkish guest-workers, and whose population is in decline, is scarcely liable to desire *Lebensraum*. Anxiety about the future of the Germans was vividly expressed in an article entitled 'Germany needs more children', in *German Comments*, spring 1990: 'the repercussions will be grave if we think of a Germany in the year 2030 with 35 million inhabitants.'

Some of our compatriots will continue to fear the idea of a new united Germany inside the European Community. Think of 80-million Germans, they will insist, with their businessmen selling computers to Ukrainians and their cars racing down the autobahns to the Crimea just as if Hitler had won the war. The answer to this is, surely, that it is a curiously un-British reaction to fear a nation because it has a large population. I have not noticed the Spanish being much in awe of the British simply because they are 40-million strong and we 58; nor was our enmity with the French in the eighteenth century based on a realisation that they had 30-million and we ten. Further, it is not as if we can wish Germany away. We can only speculate as to whether it is safer for Britain to be inside or outside a Community which includes 70 to 80 million Germans.

The other countries of Western Europe have each of them for years been well-disposed to the idea of political union. Spain, a new member of the Community, and, even by the rigid standards of General de Gaulle, a great historic nation, is entranced to be treated as part of the family of Europe after 150 years of ostracism, isolation and internal political turmoil. Liberal Spain, now firmly in power, has also always seen the road to Europe as a way to modernisation. Yet now even the Spanish Right has seen in Europe a way of enlarging the nation's sphere of action. It was an achievement of Manuel Fraga, during his years of domination of the Alianza Popular (later Partido Popular), to insist that that new party should turn warmly to the rest of Europe, rather than in on itself.

As for Italy, that nation has always seemed to have looked on the Community as a splendid, if slightly remote, grandmother, *la nonna europea*, who will compensate for the infidelities of the Italian state. 'Italians feel that they will be helped by Europe to overcome our own lack of discipline, and that has been the Italian experience', the present Italian Foreign Minister, Gianni de Michelis, told a British journalist in July 1990. 'The European process', he said, was 'associated with personal prosperity for Italians, and the promise that Europe would help Italy to improve bureaucratic efficiency'. Many Italians, after all, have come to see the nation state which their grandfathers constructed in the nineteenth century, in imitation of France, as being flawed: too small to fulfil their national genius and too large for their regional history. Mazzini assigned for Italy a unique mission (before the *Risorgimento*, of course): only a 'regenerate Italy' could initiate a new and superior life and unity. Twice before had 'the world' been united by Rome, imperial and then papal. 'Why should not a new Rome, the Rome of the Italian people . . . arise to create a third and still vaster unity – to link together and harmonise heaven and earth, right and duty . . .' No wonder there has been disillusion.

For the smaller countries of Western Europe, the Community has been a fine ride in the forest of politics whence they can at last command a view of their own futures. The governments of these states are not very sympathetic to yet another bout of national soul-searching in Britain. Their predecessors made clear-headed decisions about the Common Market in the 1950s. Some of them, too, felt a wrench at abandoning full freedom of action. Belgium may be a relatively modern state but the Netherlands is a great country, with a history of, in its time, unrivalled achievement. The Dutch have been very close to Britain and have long admired her. But even in the 1950s they were often contemptuous of Britain's clear indication that she believed that, in joining the Community, she was coming down in the world. Recently a Spanish official told me, with all the understanding of a citizen of a nation which lost the main part of its empire in the 1820s, that he believed '1992 would constitute for Britain an 1898' – the date of the intellectually creative soul-searching in Spain which followed the loss of Cuba and the Spanish-American War.

There are, we should remember, several traditions in the Continent: one is love of England; the other, deriving from Rousseau and the philosophers of the Enlightenment, is scorn for 'the stupidity of the English', and particularly the idea of our traditional, unwritten constitution deriving from feudalism – 'that iniquitous and absurd system which degrades the human race'.

Everywhere on the Continent, too, the survival of Roman law and the position of the Roman Church have preserved a state of mind where European unity is seen as something not to be created, but revived. Karl Marx correctly wrote: 'When men are about to make revolution, they fortify themselves by acting as if restoring a vanished past.' President Mitterrand, Chancellor Kohl, and Jacques Delors are, therefore, to be seen as successors of those other innovating restorers, Charlemagne and Napoleon – particularly the last, since it was he who, by channelling the positive ideas in the French Revolution towards rational reforms, created modern Europe. As Sir Lewis Namier wrote: 'he ... sapped inherited forms and loyalties, regrouped territories, established modern administrations, and familiarised tens of millions of men with change in political and social conditions – and' he added, in a typical flourish, 'new ideas are not nearly so potent as new habits.' The more or less subconscious recollection of Napoleon's 'rationalisation' survives in both Germany and Italy, even if the fall of his empire (in 1815) postponed the realisation of those rearrangements.

Thus opinion in all the capitals of continental Europe considers that the political union which the founders of the Community hoped for is not just desirable, but also possible. To those for whom Europe was the main concern, the 1980s were a time of modest progress, not retreat. The achievement of the EMS in 1979 was followed by the Genscher-Colombo proposals on European Union (1981), the Solemn Declaration of Stuttgart (1983), the Spinelli Treaty (or draft treaty) on European Union (1983), and then the Single European Act (1986). The countries which subscribed to the EMS had more success in the task of controlling inflation than those who did not. (See also Chapter X.) The old mood known as 'Europessimism' has in consequence vanished. Europe no longer considers itself a protectorate of the United States. Though Western Europe's scientific research effort is less than that of Japan and the United States, no one thinks any more that, sandwiched between the 'superpowers', Europe is impotent. Even if the Community's strength is mainly economic and civilian, not military, and looks like remaining so – whatever is done about security (see Chapter VIII) – we are living in a primarily civilian world. The European recovery from the economic crisis which began with the oil shock of 1973 has been more firmly based, many would say, than that in the United States – with more intelligent attention to the need for investment and the technological base of sustained development. The 'erosion of traditional authority in kinship, locality, language, school and other elements of the social fabric' (Robert Nisbet's words) has also been far less in Europe than in the United States.

THE IMPLICIT COMMITMENTS

The reasons for this new optimism in Europe are: the designation, largely as a result of the drive of the British Commissioner, Lord Cockfield, of 1992 as the year when the Single European Market must come finally into being; the passage of the Single European Act, abolishing the right of veto by a single government in a number of matters, thereby overcoming the apparent inertia in the political Community of the early 1980s; the coincidence of a president of France and a (French) president of the Commission who see eye to eye on the way to anchor Germany to an integrated Europe; the 'evaporation' of the Soviet threat which, by removing one of the compulsions which led to its founding, forces the Community to analyse again its *raison d'être*; and, the realisation that, in a Community of twelve, good mechanisms for common action are more necessary than in one of six - and would be even more so if there were to be further expansion of membership.

There is also the realisation that the ex-communist countries could play a great part in increasing the strength of 'Europe', provided the association with them is intelligently managed. (See also Chapter X.) An institutional discussion has been under way since the launching of the Spinelli Treaty in 1984; and, to member states which had spent so long (1979–85), haggling over the problem of the British budget, a new debate on the future of the Community seemed a good thing. Of these drives, the first, the prospect of '1992', is the most significant. Regulations, licences, restrictions, old national preferences are supposed to vanish, and we have been led to expect, at the end of that year, a new world no less remarkable, in its way, than the one whose discovery, 500 years before, we shall be marking by countless celebrations across the Continent.

III

What is Entailed

So Britain has to decide what to do about its future in a Europe which itself is on the move. We have to think hard and long, even if, as has been suggested earlier, it is against the national grain to do so. First, a word about what seems to be entailed. We do not know exactly what the continental leaders consider 'European union' to be, any more than we did in 1950. Michel Rocard, in a flash of revolutionary Gaullism, has suggested that he hopes one day to see 'a European superpower'. President Mitterrand has spoken of 'a European confederation' – perhaps stretching beyond the frontiers of the Europe of the twelve. But he has later also said, 'it doesn't matter what you call it'. More recently still, he has suggested that Europe could be 'a federation in monetary matters, and a confederation in political ones'.* In 1988, as we all

---

*El Pais, *June 26, 1990*. See also Le Monde, *June 27, 1990*: *'L'union économique et monetaire commande l'union politique, à constaté de son côté M. Mitterrand, ajoutant que cette dernière devrait avoir à termé une 'finalité fédérale'. Est-ce lá une approche nouvelle? Un moindre intérêt pour le projet de confédération présente au début de l'année? Les collaborateurs de l'Elysée le vient résolument: la fédération, expliquent-ils, c'est la Communauté de demain ou après-demain, très integrée. La confédération, quant á elle, abritera, á côté de la Communauté, ceux des pays de l'Europe jusqu'à l'Oural que ne peuvent, ou ne voulent, adhérer á le CEE.'*

remember, Jacques Delors suggested that most economic legislation would 'originate' in Brussels by the year 2000. Chancellor Kohl and Herr Pöhl have a general, if rather vague, picture of a European federation. So does Felipe González. The Italian Government 'leans to a federal model for Europe' but the evolution will be 'through a compromise between federal and confederal approaches', according to their present Foreign Minister, who added: 'In the 21st century, we shall achieve a federal Europe'. Perhaps none of these ambitions will be achieved. Yet something like them, an association which is much more than an alliance, will be under way and, early in the next century perhaps, there could indeed be a European supernation.

Obviously, there will be proposals, at the conference which began at Rome in December, for an enhancement of the powers of the European Parliament (see Chapter VII), and some suggestions for improving the relations between national parliaments and the European Council of Ministers. Perhaps that last body will be able, or required, to deal with more matters by majority voting. There will be, surely, a more serious attempt at a common foreign policy than has marked previous endeavours along those lines: Dr Kissinger used to say that 'Europe has no telephone number'. There may be some kind of European security organisation, which would mean that, in the next generation, the Europeans will be able to defend themselves without the help of the Americans – or, at least, with a much reduced American presence – as has been suggested on two occasions, by Lord Carrington. I have been long enough in the House of Lords to know that if Lord Carrington suggests an idea, it is likely to have a good chance of being put into effect. The events in the Middle East during the summer and autumn of 1990 enhance the need for such initiatives. There could even be regular meetings between European heads of state. The European Court of Justice may receive greater powers to ensure that the states put the law of the Community into effect. All these matters, and a hundred others no doubt, are on the agenda of the conference on European Union.

More important, because more precise, is the second conference, also at Rome, about monetary and economic union, to be discussed by finance ministers and official economists. But the implications of their discussions will extend far beyond the purely financial; 'monetary union is the most important political project in the Community', Mariano Rubio, the Governor of the Bank of Spain, has wisely remarked.

Assuming that these twin conferences are productive, Britain needs to consider her priorities. It seems that, when it comes to the point, the only two countries, apart from our own, with coherent policies at these meetings are France and Germany. Those countries know what they want. The rest, despite pronounced national interests, will be inclined to follow the lead of the main three. Even Spain and Italy, great nations though they are, may not do much more than adjust to the policies of the others.

One tactical difficulty for Britain about this state of affairs is that, largely because of events stretching back to the friendship of General de Gaulle and Dr Adenauer, France and Germany will be likely to present a united front. The 'heroic' friendship between those two great men was followed, after a due interval, by an even closer one between Chancellor Schmidt and President Giscard d'Estaing – as the latter's most recent book of memoirs, *L'Imagination et Le Pouvoir,* gave clear evidence. President Mitterrand and Dr Kohl are in character further apart. Yet their working relation is so good, and their joint capacity to bully (or to persuade) the continental Europeans so expert, that (despite ex-President Giscard d'Estaing's recent strictures) it seems still to be a friendship as effective as its predecessors. It is not unmoving, considered against the backcloth of European history, however inconvenient it may be to the British.

IV
Possible Policies: Withdrawal or 'Self-peripheralisation'

The issues are obviously great ones. Are there alternatives? Yes; two. The first is the idea that Britain might withdraw from Europe altogether. The second is that she might try to establish for herself a privileged position on the edge of it, whereby she might have the benefit of belonging to a customs union, but be outside the political implications of it. Let us consider these alternatives.

Withdrawal from the Community is still an honourable, even heroic, policy for patriotic Englishmen, even if it is one which no government since 1975 has seriously considered.

It is a policy which could be sustained by historical, geographical and cultural arguments. A country which has managed to avoid having either a written constitution, or a code of law, finds it a radical change to have to deal with treaties to be interpreted as if they gave us a basic law. Herein, surely, lies part of the reason for the Government's opposition to the Commission's Social Charter (and the 'Social Action Programme' based on it).

Britain has had few direct benefits from the Community – being, in this respect, different from both the original six members who founded the enterprise, and from Greece, Denmark and Ireland, which joined in the 1970s and 1980s, and whose agricultures have done well in consequence.

No British thinker made any contribution of any importance to the idea of European unity before 1945. By way of contrast, continental Europeans can recall the hopes for union of Kant or of Montesquieu. British reticence on this matter is not surprising since our European policy from the time of the Reformation, until 1950 at least, was a successful endeavour to prevent such unity, first under the auspices of Spain, then of France, finally of Germany; even though patriotic historians usually describe this policy as preserving 'the balance of power' or, as preventing 'either France or Spain from securing naval stations beyond the Straits of Dover'. Paul Johnson, author of a history of England, *The Offshore Islanders* (1972), which suggested that all that is vital in our history came from indigenous, insular roots, has since suggested that the Community cannot become a focus for British loyalties since there is no artistic or literary underpinning to it; there is neither a Goethe nor a Manzoni behind the idea of European union. But it could be argued that all English literature, from Shakespeare onwards, more than the literature of the rest of Europe, has been a preparation for a united Europe. The Romantic poets were Europeans in the broadest sense of the word; Richardson and Scott were European novelists; as was Henry James, who died an Englishman. Scottish 'Europeans' would insist, too, that their forefathers contributed fully to the European enlightenment through the work of Hume, Smith and even Burns.

What seems more discouraging is that 'Europe', as it has developed since 1945, has scarcely engaged the British intelligentsia – and who can now say that such a thing does not exist? It is not that the intelligentsia has retreated into the anti-politics of

Bloomsbury. There are great political controversies which move this section of opinion: the Government's policy towards universities, Israel, even Nicaragua, the community charge, and so on. But about the European Community, the voices of the intellectuals are strangely quiet: 'I confess I haven't given the details much thought', one (ennobled) panjandrum recently remarked to me, when I asked for his views about the proposed European currency.

One explanation is that the European issue has seemed 'too boring'; just as James Callaghan, who must have been used to surviving dull days, felt when, as Foreign Secretary, he went to Brussels 'to spend several hours discussing how to resolve our differences on standardising a fixed position of rear-view mirrors on agricultural tractors'.

Another reason is that, in the last generation, the intelligentsia has drawn closer to the United States than was the case in the past. North American universities, foundations, publishers and magazines have been peculiarly welcoming to English writers, and they have, whatever their disciplines or spheres of interest, seen the world through North Atlantic eyes (whatever their views of the North Atlantic Treaty). Many British intellectuals find the Europe of the Community as disturbing as they find the United States cosy. In that, since 1941, British governments have conceded leadership to Washington (except for Sir Anthony Eden and Edward Heath), the intelligentsia has followed its leaders.

Atlases always include the British Isles as part of Europe. But the British often slip into the usage of assuming that 'Europe' is synonymous with the Continent. 'DON'T LET EUROPE RULE BRITANNIA' ran a slogan I observed on the back of a car one summer Sunday evening near Saxmundham. 'English soccer teams let back into Europe', *The Times* announced, in its main headline, on 11 July 1990, and *The Financial Times*, than which there is no more pro-European newspaper, employed the same usage that day. 'Europe's voiceless tremors do not reach her', Keynes wrote of England in 1919, in *The Economic Consequences of the Peace*. (The whole passage reads: 'For one who spent in Paris the greater part of the six months which succeeded the Armistice an occasional visit to London was a strange experience. England still stands outside Europe. Europe's voiceless tremors do not reach her. Europe is apart and England is not of her flesh and body. But Europe is solid with herself. France, Germany, Italy, Austria, and Holland, Russia, and Roumania and Poland throb together and their structure and civilisation are essentially one.')

Then the British (why deny it, since it is a fact of history?) have had for several hundred years a proud, special view of themselves. Sir John Plumb put this well in his little book of essays, *The Death of the Past*: ' ... the vast growth of the British Empire, the fabulous wealth that poured into England in the XVIIIth and XIXth centuries, the almost constant success in battle underlined ... that England had a special destiny created for it by Providence. And even if, amongst more sophisticated minds, Providence was quietly dropped, the sense of manifest destiny was not. The Protestant martyrs were changed for English heroes Drake ... Raleigh ... Hawkins ... Clive ... Wolfe ... and beyond further back ... the same early British heroes could be discerned – Alfred, and, beyond him, Caractacus.' The English saw themselves for years as a new chosen people. In contrast, 'abroad', as King George V is supposed once to have said, was 'Hell. I know. I have been there'.

At the same time, the tugs of empire, though less strong than some continental Europeans think, certainly exist, as do those to other parts of the wider world beyond Europe. The minority of British citizens who are deeply concerned with countries other than their own are probably more interested in Africa, India, the United States, the 'white Commonwealth', and the Middle East, than they are in Europe. There is good reason: the immigrants into Britain since 1960 have mostly, after all, come from ex-imperial countries, not from our European neighbours. It is the connection of that minority with their ancient homes in India, Pakistan or the West Indies which seems the dominant factor in British relations with the outside world, not the one which we have assumed with the Continent – which is perceived widely as an August pleasure-drome, not as a place inextricably – culturally, intellectually, spiritually – connected with us.

Traditional Britain too, has a curious attitude to foreigners. Any newspaper can whip up enthusiasm, or even hatred, against the 'selfish' French or the 'bullying' Germans, the 'lazy' Spanish or the 'feckless' Italians, much easier than people in those countries can do, or do, against each other. 'Old Spanish customs' is still an expression used in the newspaper industry to indicate sloth and corrupt practice. 'Britons in Spanish prisons!' was a cry in the streets of London in 1739. It could be again in the 1990s. The controversy over Nicholas Ridley's interview to the *Spectator*, and his subsequent resignation from the cabinet in July 1990, brought out, in the correspondence columns of several newspapers, a chorus of resentful isolationism.

Of course, it is easier for people to agree on something negative than on any positive task. But this easily awakened mood of enmity is a special characteristic of Britain. It is a particularly curious manifestation, since not only is our national tradition one of tolerance but, twice in this century, we have gone to war, willingly, on behalf of a European country: Belgium in 1914, Poland in 1939. In continental Western Europe some such emotions, it is true, exist. In the nineteenth century a typical Spanish reaction was that 'England was a country of creditors' as Fortunata believed (in Pérez Galdos's *Fortunata and Jacinta*). Spanish resentment about the French harbouring Basque revolutionary terrorists is profound. I possess a brilliant squib 'Against the French' written in the style of the eighteenth century by a famous editor in Madrid, Manuel Arroyo. I dare say that many Frenchmen still think, with Stendhal, that the typical

Englishman is 'a cold, narrow-minded and honest man' (a remark made about Napoleon's surgeon at St Helena). But the vulgarity of the British tabloid press's condescension does not exist.

Relations with Germany are particularly susceptible to jingoism. Year after year, films dealing with the Second World War are shown on our television screens. Few British Christmases are complete without a revival of *Where Eagles Dare*, or *The Dambusters*. When England played Germany in the Football World Cup in 1990, *The Sun* did not hesitate to recall the war in its headline: 'Herr we go. Herr we go. We beat them in 1945. Now for 1990.' Every belligerent continental country suffered more in the Second World War than the British; yet none so consistently recalls that conflict, and never at the level of odious jocularity.

The nature of the European Community has also seemed specially difficult for the British to grasp. The Council of Ministers was initially intended to be the Community's Senate. But it is composed, nevertheless, of members of the executives of the member states. The European Parliament is not yet a legislature, and will probably never become so in the sense of being a territorial assembly, as the House of Commons has always been. What, too, is this 'Commission' in Brussels, which is neither a civil service nor a political institution? Yet it has the duty to formulate proposals for the decision of the Council of Ministers. It does not fit into our British experience, and sounds all too like that 'foreign technocracy destined to trample upon democracy' which de Gaulle castigated in a press conference of 1965. But in reality, it is less the powers of the Commission of which we should complain, than the fact that it does not have the authority which should pertain to an executive. It must depend on the Council to obtain its authority. Then the idea of the Community as a permanently moving staircase, a political escalator, 'like the river Rhine' (in Chancellor Kohl's image), with the union of the peoples a goal at the end of a long tunnel (or at the sea), is also strange to us: 'Is there ever any peace in ever climbing up the climbing wave?' we ask, with Tennyson, in *The Lotus Eaters*. The culture of the Community, with its strange, French, untranslatable words (*acquis, communautaire*) has struck no chord in British life. I am sure this is partly because, though there is now a large state sector in Britain, we have, as J. M. Lee put the matter in a speech to the Royal Historical Society in 1979, 'no equivalent of the French conception of the civil service as the robust embodiment of the state which, by centralisation, liberates the peasants from the local notables and at the same time encourages its servants to enunciate general principles of equity and organisation'. Yet the Commission at Brussels has been much influenced by this tradition. Those who have been to Brussels and come to terms with it, seem to 'have gone native' among those 'white niggers who begin at Calais' – as the playwright, Rolf Hochhuth wrote in an article in *Die Welt* at the time of the Ridley affair. Brussels, though close to the scene of Britain's greatest military victory, has always had a remote sound to us; Ronald Firbank, for the only time in his life, spoke for England when he caused one of his characters to remark, in his novel *Valmuth*, 'I can't imagine anyone going purposely to Brussels'.

There is also a psychological, or intellectual, gap between traditional British and continental approaches to problems of this kind. The traditional attitude of the Foreign Office, noticed above (Chapter I), seems to reflect the point that, since the Reformation, Anglo-Saxons have thought *a posteriori* and inductively, while the Latin peoples always think, in the tradition of Aristotle and St Thomas Aquinas, *a priori* and by deduction.

As to the practicality of a withdrawal from the Community, membership could presumably be gone back upon as a result of a vote to repeal the European Communities Act in the House of Commons. The white paper of 1971 commending accession to the Treaty of Rome stated specifically that the document contained 'no provision expressly permitting or prohibiting withdrawal... The Community... rests on the original consent, and hence on the continuing consent, of member states and, hence, of national parliaments'. The Community has no armed force to prevent secession. Assuming that the spirit of fair play survived (as surely it would if there is to be such a reassertion of English (and British) values as this policy implies), a new referendum to test opinion might seem necessary, and the 'Europeans' might again win. But if they did not, the way for withdrawal would be open.

No one, it is true, could be sure, in such circumstances, what would become of the body of European law which has become our law since 1973. But there are many lawyers who would, for a sensible fee, unravel things – to the applause of more than the English fishermen who thought themselves outmanoeuvred in 1990 by the action of the European court in permitting some of their Spanish *confrères* to fish under British flags of convenience until the matter at issue was finally resolved. Nor would the rolling up of the map of the Common Agricultural Policy seem painful, though there are other European programmes – including fisheries, for example – which it might seem more disadvantageous to abandon.

Other consequences of such action might be harsh. Both business and (after Jacques Delors' visit to their annual Congress in 1988) trade unions have geared themselves to the completion of the Single Market of 1992, so that a break for 'freedom', as some would represent it, might be disintegratory. The enthusiasm of the stock market for Britain's participation in the exchange rate mechanism of the European monetary system in 1990 was a sign of the City of London's expectations. Companies have, after all, not waited on the completion of legislation by the Community to prepare themselves for the Single Market. The last few years have seen 'an explosion of restructuring, rationalisation and international diversification without precedent in Europe's industrial history'. Bankers assume that the Single Market is here: the volume of business conducted between European-based banks in the first nine months of 1989 was more than double the volume for the whole preceding year. According to *The Financial Times*, 'many of the institutional changes shaping that [the Single Market] are already in place'. Withdrawal might ruin the City; one cannot say anything less.

It is also possible that Scotland, and even Wales, might, if the choice were posed to them, choose to remain, with Ireland, in the European Community. So the United Kingdom might at last break up.

The Commonwealth would offer no haven to a newly de-Europeanised Britain. Its members have in general made their own arrangements (some, indeed, with the European Community) which they would not wish to abandon. As Harold Macmillan wrote in 1963 in his diary, 'had there been a chance of a Commonwealth Free Trade area, we should have grasped it years ago'.

The Community members who are also members of NATO will one day probably associate themselves in some kind of new European Defence Community, as suggested earlier (Chapter VIII), and as even the communiqué at the NATO meeting in London proposed in July 1990. The members of EFTA who are seeking a special arrangement with the Community by way of the so-called European Economic Space may participate. The strategic consequences of withdrawal could thus also be considerable.

Over half of Britain's trade is now with the countries of the Community. But she could find herself facing a reimposition of non-tariff barriers. At best, she would be dealing, in her own geographical zone, with an economic power which, even if positive and benign (which could not be quite assured), she might not be able to influence.

British ministers and officials would presumably have to continue going backwards and forwards to Brussels and other

European capitals; but, if they did so, they would no longer be going in the guise of commanders from outlying garrisons of a resuscitated Roman Empire, but more as leaders of barbarian tribes, kept waiting in anterooms, and excluded from the main decision-making.

No doubt, in these circumstances, Britain could count on sympathy in the United States. Yet official America, ever since President Kennedy's speech at Philadelphia in 1962, has for long supported a united Europe. President Bush's administration has given more support to the idea of European integration than any since that of Kennedy. William Taft, the United States ambassador to NATO (an ex-Under Secretary for Defence), has approved the idea of the European Community investigating the possibilities of security arrangements. In 1959–60, United States interest in the European Economic Community, rather than EFTA, was one reason for Harold Macmillan himself turning to the former. In future, too, a United States, with every year a larger Hispanic population, is likely to be focusing such attention as it can afford on external matters, on Mexico, Central America and the Pacific, as well as on the Middle East. Anglo-Saxon loyalties, deriving from the common ancestry of ourselves and their founding fathers, our law and our literature, will, of course, survive in the United States. But they will probably be every year less strong. It is true that the crisis in the Persian Gulf has enhanced the idea of British collaboration with the United States. But the change may be ephemeral.

The United States, after all, will soon be in search of a new world posture. Her dedication to an active foreign policy has, since 1945, depended on the perceived emergency of the 'communist threat'. If there is no threat, there may be no policy. Already in December 1989, the United States appeared to George Steiner 'a provincial colossus, ignorant of, indifferent towards, Europe'. Culturally, economically and spiritually, Britain would certainly be drawn more and more towards the

United States in the event of a rejection of Europe. A 'dollarisation' of our economy might follow; it is already close. The rhythm of our daily life is today adjusted to that of the United States. As François Mauriac put it in one of his famous *Bloc Notes* in *L'Express*, on the eve of a visit from a president of the United States to Paris: 'Their music orchestrates our days with millions of records. Thousands of films ... impose their style on us in every way.' These remarks are even more applicable to Britain in the 1990s when, thanks chiefly to the influence of our monolingual, comfortably lowbrow television, Britain's cultural connections with the Continent are less than they used to be.

If Britain today were a rich, hard-working, patriotic, well-educated, self-sufficient nation, ready for sacrifice, as well as disdainful of comfort – a Singapore, say, of the North Sea – a policy of withdrawal from the European Community might lead to national regeneration. Since we are, however, not now obviously all those things, the choice of liberty could also lead to national disaster. Merry England might turn out to be further away than ever. Internal feuds might replace foreign adventures.

The curious thing, though, about a vision of our future relations with Europe which suggests withdrawal is that practically no public personality now openly supports it; not even, apparently, Mr Enoch Powell. But some leader writers, such as the accomplished Peregrine Worsthorne of *The Sunday Telegraph*, write as if such a policy represents their dream (Mr Worsthorne has even accused those who disagree with him on this subject, of treason). They might consider, surely, whether, as they mock the '*bien pensants*', the 'good and great', who they see as leading the country to perdition (yet again), they ought not to support more openly this position of withdrawal to which their arguments point.

A second policy, and again the Government has opposed it (though it could be reconsidered), is one where we would maintain our membership of the Community in so far as it remains an economic or customs union, including the Single Market of 1992 (which the present Government has done much to prepare), but refuse further measures of both monetary and political union. This argument has been put best, with eloquence, by Oliver Letwin, of Rothschild's Bank, in a paper published in the autumn of 1989. Many other commentators write as if they would like to see this consummation.

Again, this is a possible policy. It is not dishonourable – even though it would run contrary to Britain's solemn declarations, and certainly ignores the spirit of the Treaty of Rome. It also has logic if considered against our historical way of doing things. Jean Monnet said of us: 'Their national character inclines them to seek a special position, which will save them from having to change.' The creation of EFTA was one (unsuccessful) manifestation of this. So was British reluctance, and then agreement 12 years later, fully to join the European Monetary System.

There would be disadvantages: European law applies to all countries which are members of the Community and is applied instantly. It would be difficult to negotiate a position where we could pick and choose those laws which we liked, and those which we did not. We might also feel a little lonely, since several of the six nations now in the free trade area (Austria certainly; perhaps Switzerland, Norway and Sweden, though presumably not Finland or Iceland) may seek entry to the Community during the 1990s. 'Most Swedes', we were told in *The Financial Times* on 3 July 1990 'do not really like what is happening. They would prefer that Europe adjusted to them. But the more sensible accept that they have no real choice. In practice, this means Sweden must become a full member of the European Community. Increasingly, the question is not if, but when . . .' The same may, in the end, be said in some of the other countries. (Thus Finland's trade is about 50 per cent with The Community.) Austria's application, like that of Turkey, will anyway be considered in 1993.

POSSIBLE POLICIES

We should, with a policy such as is here suggested, find, as in the case of withdrawal, our economy heavily influenced, or determined, by the decisions of continental Europeans over whom we would have no control and whom we could not formally influence. Karl Otto Pöhl, President of the Bundesbank, would still be with us, only we should not expect him to come to see us often; we should have to visit him.

Still, we have plainly not heard the last of this approach. It does not seem far away from the thinking of Nicholas Ridley, the former Secretary of State for trade and industry. A free vote of the House of Commons might even now support it. That body may, in respect of Europe, have changed less from what it seemed to be in 1961, in the estimate of the late Maurice Macmillan, than is often assumed.

The idea is also one which could easily be combined with other schemes under consideration in both Germany and France. These envisage a two-tier Europe, the first tier to consist of a core of states willing to proceed fast to full monetary union, and so to political union; and the second tier to imply an outer rim of nations reluctant to abandon sovereignty or in some other way as yet still 'unripe' in the minds of the Germans and French, for living in Europe. Herr Pöhl has said that Europe 'should not wait for the last ship in the convoy'. These last ships might include, as well as Britain, Spain, Greece, Ireland, and the nations of EFTA. They might be joined, eventually, by the ex-communist countries of central Europe – those countries which have miraculously, or so it seems, become, in the last year, free of Russian dominance, and which will wish to be associated with the Community eventually. (See Chapter VIII.)

It has also been said that Herr Pöhl in truth hopes that Britain, as well as Spain, will, instead, be in this inner circle, leaving out only Portugal and Greece among present members of the Community. There is some ambiguity. But there is none about the fact that the prospect of German and French pressure for monetary union, leading to two tiers, has disturbed the Bank of Spain as much as it has the Bank of England. Still, such a plan, has a history: Monnet, for example, thought that the unity of Europe would begin with the unification of France and Germany, and that others would join in later.

The chances of the emergence of such a Europe of two speeds, or of 'variable geometry', seem more likely after the agreement, in June 1990, at Schengen, a tiny river village in Luxembourg, by the original six members of the first Community (except for Italy) to move to abolish all border controls. If the borders of 'Schengenland' were to coincide with those of the European Monetary Union, the prospect of a 'core Europe' which excluded Britain (and perhaps Italy and Spain) would be enhanced. Most people believe that such a conclusion would very definitely not be to our benefit.

Opposition to such a relegation to the second tier does not imply that the entire Community should always proceed together: 'There may be certain areas where it makes sense for one or two countries to develop bilateral arrangements, even if the rest of the Community is not doing the same', Malcolm Rifkind rightly told the Select Committee of the House of Lords in 1985. But a development of two camps within the Community would be to risk the whole notion of 'community' and would certainly work to the disadvantage of the excluded members.

* * *

Both these policies, withdrawal and 'self-peripheralisation', can be presented either as maintaining the *status quo*, or as preserving a historically justifiable position. But both in fact really assume a new historical placing; for, ever since 1961, British statesmen have seen a satisfactory place in Europe as the object of their international policy. Before 1961, and since the seventeenth century, Britain – England – was an imperial power. No useful purpose can be served by making comparisons with the sixteenth century. Thus, what the 'anti-Europeans' insist on as being a *status quo*, would turn out to be unfamiliar terrain. The novelty in practice sought by such traditionalists would be, perhaps, in keeping with a nation which since the outbreak of war in 1939 (perhaps since 1914), has gone to great efforts to avoid facing reality. Thus we concealed the loss of Empire from ourselves by devising the subterfuge of the Commonwealth, which seems now little more than a sports club. We were able to look on ourselves as a great victor in 1945, when in fact we had lost much of our international strength (if not our standing). We even represented Suez as a triumph.

V

The Need to Devise a Frame: Sovereignty, Union, Federation, Confederation

The two choices, for a withdrawal and for a special position, seem thus likely to be to our disadvantage; perhaps even to our grave disadvantage.

We should, therefore, though recognising the psychological change which will be needed, reconcile ourselves to entering upon the discussions at both the current inter-governmental conferences, on the one hand, with a determination to see that our suggestions for the European future are presented well, but, on the other hand, with a realisation that we may have to accept, at least for the moment, plans which we will have argued against.

Earlier, I recalled the importance of not neglecting the one-third of Britain who voted 'no' in the referendum of 1975. But those who voted 'yes' constituted two-thirds of the electorate. They must be presumed to have pondered these things: 'ever closer union', as well as the promised 'Community of Nations'.

We should, therefore, also as a nation, take a deep breath,

collectively but rationally, and realise that we are already part of something which is more than an alliance or a customs union. We must insist that the country did indeed make the decision to belong to a European Union in the 1960s and 1970s. The distinction between the Community as a political union and a customs union may then have been blurred, less deliberately than through our national reluctance to think ahead. There was surely no deception. But there may have been self-deception. There is a precedent for such an approach. For even the Empire was achieved, according to Professor Seeley, in his inaugural lecture at the University of Cambridge in 1869, in 'a fit of absence of mind'. So it may be with European Union.

The Government, until recently, has rationally insisted that it is inappropriate and unnecessary, even unwise, to think ahead about such things, and that it would be best to wait until the projected Single Market is complete in 1992 or 1993 before even discussing the next stage. That policy, as has been observed earlier in this essay, has all the elements of good 'Monnetism'.

All the same, in the more expectant mood of Europe of the 1990s, such pragmatism has come to seem inadequate. Margaret Thatcher, in a document tabled at the Summit of Stuttgart in 1984, included as a European objective that of trying to 'heighten the consciousness among our citizens of what unites us'. There is a time for rhetoric and a time for vision, just as there is a time to discuss the size of tomatoes.

At this stage, I hear beyond my window the well-known call of the patriotic members of the House of Commons: 'Sovereignty, sovereignty'. But that allusion is to a concept, serviceable in its time which, in an absolute sense, has surely outlived its usefulness. It was devised to express the thought that the modern state (as opposed to the Church or to local authorities) ought to have supreme authority. The idea is Roman in origin: the state as an absolute as described by Cicero – ' a *populus* welded together by a bond of *law* into a corporate body with supreme legal authority'. The sixteenth-century French philosopher, Jean Bodin, claimed to have defined this idea first. In fact, he revived it. In the 1560s the moment was propitious for Bodin. The mediaeval order was in ruins. The new model ruler was seen to be limited neither by the laws of the Pope and Church, nor by those of the Emperor; certainly not by the rights of a feudal tenant-in-chief.

Four hundred years later, the notion of sovereignty, as a synonym for supreme power vested in the state, has weakened. Since the formation of the United Nations in 1945 (or since the formation of the League of Nations in 1919), the majority of civilised states have regarded their freedom of action as limited under the Charter (or, before it, the Covenant). Since the formation of NATO in 1949, the member states have recognised that they could not defend themselves against their most likely enemy unless they were permanent members of an alliance. International economic activity, including investment, credit and loans, has transformed the nation state's operations in another sphere of action. So has the European Community, even if it is still customary to insist that what has happened has been 'an abnegation of *exclusive* sovereignty in a limited field where the Community exercised the *collective* sovereignty of the member states'.

The British public was often reminded of these things between 1961 and 1975. I have quoted Lord Home's statement in August 1961. Harold Macmillan, at the 1961 Conservative Conference, admitted 'going in [to Europe] must involve some pooling of national freedom of action'. He also said elsewhere that sovereignty was 'in the end, perhaps a matter of degree'.

In 1914, Britain, Spain, France and Germany were sovereign states as well as nations. Scotland, Catalonia, and (perhaps) Bavaria were nations, but they were not states and so had no sovereignty. By 1990, the twelve nation states of the Community had abandoned their sovereignty in the old sense. The original six members of the Community did that (not without bitter debate in France, above all) in 1957; Britain in 1973. Each still has considerable freedom of action. We have more control over our destinies than if we had remained a sovereign state, as Norway has done after its referendum on the Community in 1975. But we do not have sovereignty as we had it before 1973. We have what the present French Socialist spokesman on Europe, Gerard Fuchs, has described as 'collective mastery of our own destiny'. The truth is that sovereignty today has no more to it than, to quote Lord Hervey in a slightly different context, 'the long-fled bloom of a last century toast'.

We should now reflect upon what sort of Europe, within, to be sure, the bounds of possible choices, we do wish to see – while not falling into the trap of thinking that we can still discuss whether or no there should be a European Community at all. As a Chinese proverb favoured by Chou En-lai has it: 'The helmsman must guide the boat by using the waves; otherwise it will be submerged by the waves.' If we do not know what we want, we shall achieve nothing. Worse, we shall be outmanoeuvred by those who do have plans, however unsatisfactory to us. We can easily, with a little imagination, see in our mind's eye how a Europe framed entirely by French *polytechniciens* might turn out. If we were to stand quite aside, such a thing might easily occur. No one would get anywhere unless they could pass examinations. European *grandes écoles* might dominate us all. Yet assuming that we remain even partially a member of the Community, we would find ourselves being influenced, or determined, by such things.

Western Europe now constitutes a 'Community'. That word, even if Jean Monnet thought he had invented it, is imprecise. 'The Community' is always being used to describe people gathered together in some amorphous political unit with no firm territorial basis. Gladstone used the word in 1888 to describe the old Concert of Europe: 'We are part of the Community of Europe and must do our duty as such.' 'Union' may seem to mean more than 'Community'. The Union of England and Scotland (1707) meant, and has signified, a close association. The Union of Kalmar was a union of crowns in Scandinavia which lasted, uneasily, a hundred years but then broke up. The United States (of America) is a union. 'Will Texas join the Union?' people asked in 1840; and, in 1850, 'will Cuba?' On the European continent, the word 'union' appears to mean less. We have been part of the Western European 'Union' since 1948, for the purposes of defence, without allowing it noticeably to affect us. The Select Committee of the House of Lords in 1985 meekly said: 'Insofar as it is possible to offer a definition at all, 'European Union' implies a greater degree of political integration among the nation states of Europe than exists at present' – a conclusion which had a really august banality.

Two words to describe the association which the Community either is, or may become, are 'Confederation' and 'Federation'. The first may be what the Community already constitutes: a permanent union of sovereign states, drawn together for common purposes. I have quoted Harold Macmillan several times – appropriately, since he was the Prime Minister who sprang the game at Britain's European *battue*, a metaphor which he might have liked. Macmillan, in his speech commending membership of the Community to the House of Commons, in 1961, said that 'confederation' was a concept 'in tune with the national traditions of European countries and in particular of our own. It is one with which we could associate willingly and wholeheartedly'. Dr David Owen recently said much the same: 'I have no intention whatever of losing the concept of a confederation of nation states.' On the other hand, the Minister of State at the Foreign Office in 1985, Malcolm Rifkind, said: 'We are dealing not with a federation *nor a confederation* [my italics] but with a community of nation states who [*sic*] have pooled a certain amount of sovereignty.'

In the United States, the word 'confederation' indicated the association between the ex-colonies such as it was, until 1789.

The word 'federation' was then introduced, implying a closer union, with a common government. The German Confederation (*Bund*), a very loose association indeed, established at the Congress of Vienna in 1815, was another such association. The word is less precise than it seems. Switzerland is officially 'the Swiss Confederation'. Yet it is a federation – with a weak central authority. West Germany was – and newly united Germany is – a federal republic with a stronger central authority than that of Switzerland. Mexico is formally a federal republic. In practice, it is a strong, over-centralised state.

'Federation' has, in fact, come to mean a union of states (or provinces) in which there is a common government, to which the member states have agreed to delegate certain powers and functions. The separate states retain their individual sovereignty so far as the residue of powers unallotted to the central or federal authority is concerned.

The European Community, speaking simplistically, is already somewhere between a 'confederation' of nation states and a 'federation'. We may not be within sight of a European government in the usual sense of that term. But at the same time, the states have abandoned much of their freedom of action – agricultural policy being the obvious thing which is surrendered. Roy Jenkins told the Select Committee of the House of Lords that he thought Europe would develop something neither 'strictly federalist nor confederalist according to the textbooks'. Sir Geoffrey Howe has said much the same: 'The European Community is really quite unlike any other arrangement between states that has gone before. That unique quality is one reason perhaps for its unique success.' Nevertheless, those who fear the very concept of federation may be assured: the word can indicate a proper division of responsibilities between a central authority (which might have a modest power, as was the case in the United States between 1789 and 1861), and a series of devolved authorities (which could have strong powers). With or without subscribing to a name previously used, we should work just as hard at devising a way of ensuring the devolution, or retention, of powers, as of establishing Community decision-making. Otherwise we – the Europeans as a whole, not just the British – could find ourselves facing exessive power concentrated at the centre.

In respect of external policy, the Foreign Office has defined its aims in terms which would not sound different if they were serving a federal state: 'We . . . want unity in dealing with the outside world; a Europe united in its approach to external policy, which not only consults together but acts together and is seen by others as a cohesive political entity.' (The notion of 'subsidiarity' is discussed in Chapter VI.)

The search for a description of what is already, anyway, called a 'Union' as well as a 'Community' is, I have come to think (along with many others who have studied the matter) a mistake. The achievement of a single market, together with some of the things suggested as desirable in Chapters VI to XI, will indicate more plainly what those words mean. Most of the other words which might be used frighten some sections of opinion, without satisfying any particular need.

All the same, given the way that the European debate has developed, and given the continuing proud mood of the House of Commons, some artifice may be needed to ensure that Britain will be able to participate fully in all these far-reaching experiments. The approach must be, I think, that the Government must always be able to reassure the House of Commons that the nation's membership of the Community could be rescinded by repealing the European Communities Bill. That would preserve for Britain the illusion of sovereignty. In practice, the repeal will never happen. It would be an event comparable to the Queen sending for the Duke of Norfolk to form a government; or, to point to a more obvious parallel, to Texas exercising its formal right to secede from the United States. But though we believe ourselves to be a practical nation, we need illusions. Perhaps a Bill along these lines should be ritually introduced every year as an appendix to The Queen's Speech opening Parliament. The ceremony could be made as elaborate as the threat would be unreal. Continental Europeans should understand the need for this – both because of their understanding of the importance of ceremony, and because of the admiration which most have had for British liberty in the past.

The frame to be found for Europe should, name or no name, be the focus of a supplementary loyalty to what we (all of the members, not just ourselves) have already to the nation state. It need not be a higher loyalty; a Welshman is loyal, I suspect, first to Wales and then to Britain. Sophisticated people for many generations have sustained the idea that they have many loyalties: family, locality, region, nation, cause perhaps (for example, 'the West', or Manchester United), and, of course, the Church. 'The European identity should not replace the national identity', a member of the European Parliament, George Sutra de Germa, told the House of Lords in 1975, 'it is a supplement to it'. Such diversity of loyalty is one of the ways that a free society differs from a totalitarian one.

The nature of our European attachment may, in fact, turn out to be comparable in practice to the idea of our relation with the Roman Church before the Reformation. In the Middle Ages, before the age of the nation state much less of nationalism, 'metropolitans', or archbishops, would always go to Rome to receive their pallium. In respect of fundamental beliefs, the nations of Europe were united. In the twenty-first century, we shall expect to go to Brussels (or to another capital if it seems right) to determine the guidelines of economic policy, and of whatever other things are decided to be in the zone of operation of the Community. On other matters, we would seek, and maintain, a freedom of action infinitely greater than that which the national churches had before the Reformation. When, in the 1960s, continental Europeans joked that General de Gaulle was 'the

Emperor', while the President of the European Commission, Dr Walter Hallstein, was 'the Pope', they may have been closer to the likely development of the Continent than they realised. Ulstermen and others may not find this analogy reassuring. All the same, it has force.

An important change in respect of whatever is decided about the requirements indicated in this chapter is this: it is increasingly inappropriate for the affairs of the Government with other Europeans to be dealt with by the 'Foreign Office' – or the 'Foreign and Commonwealth Office'. Foreign affairs should be redefined as relations which the nation has with nation states which are not members of the Community. There should be established a special Ministry for Europe which, freed from the Foreign Office's institutional reluctance to look far ahead and to plan, would be able to attend to the subtleties indicated in this chapter with undivided attention. 'Ambassadors' within the Community too should lose that title. They should be re-named 'Residents', and take their place by the side of High Commissioners. Names and words mean little, it may be said, but they indicate unspoken assumptions. As I have earlier insisted, Europe, in the mansion of officialdom, should now be seen as being on a floor between domestic and external relations.

VI
Subsidiarity

To determine the different levels of national and Community responsibility is the most significant matter for the conference on political union. The critical word in this debate is, as we all have now learned, 'subsidiarity'. The Oxford Dictionary dates this term to a papal encyclical of 1931. Those who are sceptical of anything emanating from Rome should be reassured; the first use of the idea of representation with full powers, the essential element in modern parliamentary life, has been derived from practices of the Roman Church in the late Middle Ages. The Institute of Directors dislikes the word since it argues that the zones of operation of the nation state are subsidiary to those which will be controlled by Europe. That is to be guarded against. But it will not necessarily be the case.

Whatever our doubts about the word, which is as ugly as most of those emanating from the European Community, the concept of subsidiarity is the decisive one in our pursuit of establishing a proper balance between national and European lines of competence and responsibility. Otto von Habsburg, MEP, has suggested that there should be a new treaty on this subject. That is a good idea, for, as Ferdinand Mount has rightly written, the relations between Britain and the other nations of Europe are being damaged by the continuing uncertainty as to what is likely in future to be within the competence of the Community, and what is likely to be within that of the nation. The same could easily happen in other countries. Thus I read in the Spanish newspaper *ABC* in April last the following news item: '*Manzanócratas* [i.e., Apple-ocrats]. The Bureaucracy of Brussels is reaching unimaginable lengths. If you like small apples, prepare to get cross. The European Commission has decreed that the European farmers cannot sell to the public apples which are smaller than 55 millimetres.'

In 1989, I gave a speech at the Fiesta de Santa Tecla in Tarragona, which I entitled 'A Europe of Diversity'. After recalling the patronal saint's exemplary conduct in difficult circumstances towards the end of the Roman Empire, I tried to insist that, where the British were seen by some continental Europeans as unenthusiastic about Europe, they should be seen as being concerned to save the whole of Europe from the fate which overtook Spain during the centralist regime of General Franco, when even the use of the Catalan language was for a time frowned on, and was never exhibited on the names of streets and even shops. Afterwards, Mgr Torroella, the Archbishop of Tarragona, a learned prelate who had been many years in Rome, agreed with me: 'Exactly,' he said, 'we must be united but not absorbed. That is the principle which we are trying to fulfil in relation to the Anglican Church.'

Goethe, who surely should always be recalled in an essay about Europe, made this same point in 1830 when talking to Eckerman of German unity (which he favoured): 'if we imagine that the unity of Germany consists in . . . having a single great capital, and that this one great capital would conduce to the development of great individual talent, or to the welfare of the great mass of people – we are in error . . . whence is Germany great, but by the admirable culture of the people which equally pervades all parts of the Kingdom? . . . Frankfurt, Bremen, Hamburg and Lübeck are great and brilliant; their effect on the prosperity of Germany is incalculable. But would they remain what they are if they lost their own sovereignty and became incorporated with any great German kingdom as provincial towns? I see reason to doubt.'

The subjects which we might consider as belonging to the realm of the Community would presumably include (and I mention them in no particular order) first, of course, those things to which the existing treaties apply: namely, measures to ensure the free movement of goods, persons, services and capital, and competition; agriculture and fisheries – also already under the direction of the Community; economic co-ordination, including the organisation of such currency or monetary union as is agreed; then, the environment; co-ordination of aid to the ex-communist countries; probably, at least at one level, defence and security, though the forum for them would have to be carefully considered (see Chapter VIII); perhaps immigration, which may turn out to be a matter of special concern; transport, at least at the international level; perhaps energy. Some would like to see posts and telegraphs, as well as telephones, Europeanised as soon as possible. Indeed, the concept of 'Europeanisation', as opposed to nationalisation, may well have a future.

Of these issues, immigration could turn out to be one of the most intractable. On the one hand, there is the attraction of the Community for people from the ex-communist countries. Already Italian and Spanish companies and bourgeoisie hire Polish butlers and Czech masons. Romanian refugees throng the streets of Berlin. Beyond the river Bug, the numbers of potential refugees in the event of a breakdown of order in the Soviet Union are virtually limitless; even now Moscow is thronged by refugees from the Caucasus.

On the other hand, the long coastlines of both Spain and Italy provide harbours as seductive as Circe's to hundreds of thousands of African or Middle Eastern immigrants. Until 1990,

Italy, a country traditionally of emigrants, had no law on immigration. The first such was inspired by, first, the appreciation that Florentines and Romans were protesting against the presence among them of these new 'invaders', and, second, because there were already over a million immigrants in Italy from the Mahgreb. Spain has also become a target for immigrants from Morocco: the country, previously sheltered since the sixteenth century from racial disturbances, has discovered prejudice. France already has a substantial and permanent minority of North Africans, who have turned several French suburbs into Muslim zones, and have inspired Jean Le Pen's National Front. Behind the existing immigrants lie the exploding North African populations: there will be 100-million people there by the year 2000. Of these 60 per cent will be under 20 years of age, and many will be unemployed. These factors have only to be named to be appreciated as potentially explosive. Italy's entry into the Schengen group of countries (the abolition of border controls) was made contingent on its making controls on entry from outside the Community similar to those existing in 'Schengenland'. For the residents of the slums of the Mahgreb, 'Europe' is a delectable golf course, with a generally declining population which in future will probably need to import more and more labour.

On the other hand, the subjects which, presumably, all governments would wish to keep in the national domain will probably include education; health; the formation of budgetary policy; and taxation (except for indirect taxation). Policies towards sport, including hunting, shooting and bullfights, policies towards the arts and the media, should also be nationally reserved. If the shooters of doves in the Médoc want to maintain their sport, or the Spanish to maintain indefinitely their *fiesta nacional*, bullfighting, it should be no concern of anyone in Brussels or Strasbourg. It is easy to imagine a busybody in the Rue de la Loi seeking to ban smoking throughout Europe. The idea should be resisted. If Spain wishes to restrain her citizens from selling their El Grecos to a German millionaire, she should be entitled to do so, even though such an entitlement would clash with the Community's requirement for an open market.

A clear, detailed and carefully constructed British policy on 'subsidiarity' would be welcomed in many of the nations of the Twelve, and might easily be supported by other governments among them. A Europe of diversity, not a centralised one, is, after all, desired by nearly all thinking people in the continental countries. A light central authority, accompanied by substantial national reserved areas, is what most Europeans desire. Considering how the nations of Europe have lost so many of their national customs over the last century, and began doing so long before the foundation of the Community, a programme for the maintenance of individuality might turn out to be as important as one for harmonisation. In relation to Spain, this point was made rather well by the Algerian leader Ahmed Ben Bella, who is re-emerging as a potential statesman: 'I have the impression that you are losing your distinctness in integrating with Europe. A pity. Spain has a special scent, a wonderful scent. Be good Europeans, but keep that scent.'

The ideas of Max Streibl, Prime Minister of Bavaria, for a Europe of regions ('a three-tier decision-making structure in a future Europe') have much to commend them too. Jordi Pujol, president of the Generalitat of Cataluña, has the same ideas. Although obviously difficult to put into effect now in unitary states, such as France and Britain, there is no reason why such ideas should not be introduced in those which are not. Here Malcolm Rifkind's policy, expressed earlier (see Chapter IV), could well be broadened to become the guide for a major institutional reform. Of course, there are difficulties: there is, for example, a small slice of old Silesia which after 1945 remained part of Germany. It is now resisting incorporation into Saxony as one of the new *Länder* in a united Germany. 'Europeanist' slogans have appeared, such as 'Görlitz with European dimensions' – Görlitz being the biggest city in the region concerned.

I do not wish to complicate my argument by straying here into the question of British constitutional reform; but, in the long run, both Britain and France could do worse than look again at their institutional arrangements for regional government. De Gaulle, it is true, allowed himself to be defeated on this subject; and the Conservatives spent an unconscionably long time dealing with the metropolitan authorities in the 1980s. But in a world which is everywhere seeing the revival of regional traditions, as well as of international associations, these things should be re-examined; and to do so in the context of Europe might be the best approach. There is no reason for uniformity – nor any reason to think such a policy should, in Britain, be the monopoly of Liberals. The autonomous governments in Spain, like the *Länder* in Germany, were all supported by the equivalent of Conservatives. There are four autonomous governments in modern Spain (Cataluña, the Basque country, Andalucia and Valencia), which control education and where the authority of the national Minister for Education is confined to remote supervision; in the other autonomous regions the old central authority in respect of those things survives. Regional governments are always expensive but, in a short time, they have often made a considerable impact on both the economic and the cultural lives of the regions concerned: Germany and Spain prove it. Major parties in Britain should reconsider the notion.

VII

European Democracy

Britain, the 'mother of Parliaments', will presumably want to make a special insistence, at the proposed conference on political union, on the evolution of the European Parliament. The 'democratic deficit' is a serious matter in the Community, even if the phrase, suggesting a modest overdraft at some provincial bank, is yet another inadequate one. It has always been the case that 'the concentration of decision-making... in the hands of the Council of Ministers and a non-elected Commission is ... undemocratic'. The 'deficit' has grown since the passage of the Single European Act. Until then, the Community's decisions had to be taken by a unanimous vote of the member states. Members of national legislatures were able to persuade themselves, at least, that, through the use of their minister's veto, they could supervise what went on in the Community. Since 1987 national ministers can be outvoted in the Council of Ministers by their colleagues. So the legally binding decisions of that body are now beyond the reach of national parliaments. David Martin, MEP, has tartly commented: 'if the European Community were a state, and applied to join the Community, it would be turned down on the grounds that it was not a democracy.'

The aim of a parliament is usually two-fold: to check the activity of the executive; and to start legislation. But in the European Community, it is not clear what is to be checked. Overall responsibility for decisions in the Community is hard to tie down. Presumably, ultimate responsibility lies with the European Council, that is, the heads of government. Individually, these men and women are responsible to their national parliaments and electorates. But, collectively, they answer to nobody. The same is true of the Council of Ministers – whether it be seen as a caucus of foreign ministers or of other ministers. The Commission can be collectively dismissed by the Parliament, but it has never happened. Nor does the Parliament in Strasbourg inspire legislation.

Many ideas have been canvassed to meet these and other institutional weaknesses. The summit at Dublin in June 1990 defined 'political union' as a means of transforming the Community into a polity which would be 'under the effective control of elected politicians'. President Mitterrand has suggested a President of the Council of Ministers to last two or three years, though it is not clear how he would be nominated. Douglas Hurd wants 'stronger powers for the European Parliament and Court of Auditors to ensure stricter financial control and counter fraud'. Perhaps there is a way to make coherent the link between the Council of Ministers and national parliaments. Vernon Bogdanor, of Oxford, wants Europe-wide referenda, and the direct election of the President of the Commission. David Martin, MEP, proposes a federal parliamentary state, in which the Parliament would explicitly share legislative powers with the Council of Ministers: the European Parliament could then initiate legislation and elect the President of the Commission as well as dismiss individual Commissioners. William Cash, MP, an opponent of federalism, would like to see closer examination of European Community policy by governments, and less secrecy in the Council. Alan Sked, of the London School of Economics, wants a European cabinet responsible to the Parliament. His parliament would, however, be composed of delegations of national parliaments, while his cabinet would be composed of men and women chosen by national governments. Other ideas are in the air – even if the air is only, as ever, that rarefied air breathed in Westminster, Brussels and Strasbourg. I wonder myself whether we will take the European Parliament seriously (or that it will take itself seriously?) until we have given it some tax-gathering powers. Clearly the new Germany requires several more members of the European Parliament. Why should Britain not propose it, since we welcome the democratisation of East Germany?

I have two further modest institutional suggestions for the European Parliament. First, the status of MEPs might, throughout Europe, be enhanced by arranging that, let us say, a quarter of them should become, in order of seniority, members of the upper house of the national legislature. Thus they could, for example, supplement the bishops in the House of Lords.

Second, the Parliament and the institutions of the Community should, of course, all be brought together in one place. There might be, as the 'Action Committee for a United States of Europe' suggested in 1957, some kind of 'federal district'. It should not be in a capital. Brussels is inadequate. The buildings of 'Europe' should have style. Magnificence is not necessary. Nobility is. Turin might be the ideal place, though Strasbourg has many merits: the Parliament building is already on an island made by canals.

But these ideas are less important than ensuring that the European Parliament acquires, in future, the vitality, responsibility, effectiveness and drive that characterises a real parliament. That is, it must become a legislature. That in turn necessitates a revision of the other institutions of the Community since the Council of Ministers was intended to be the Senate of Europe, as well as being the effective executive of the Community.

There are three more critical points: first, the Parliament should limit itself, and its zone of operation, as well as extend its powers. That is, it should be entitled to discuss only those matters which had been allocated to the sphere of the Community by the Treaty of Subsidiarity. If an MEP wished to raise the matter of bullfights, for example, he must (assuming the treaty takes the form which I have suggested in Chapter VI) be ruled out of order. The Parliament must, furthermore, enter into argument and, if necessary, be ready to challenge the European Court of Justice to ensure that European legislation is considered by Parliament and not just by the Court.

The second point is that, where the Treaty of Subsidiarity has allocated to the Community a major role, the Parliament should make itself an effective legislature. The European Council's decisions, the decisions of the Council of Ministers, the proposals of the Commission, should all be seen to have to pass through the Parliament before they become law. The Parliament should have the last word. A third role might be played by the Parliament in approving or rejecting national governments' proposals for Commissioners; that is similar to what happens with cabinet members and certain other officials in the United States.

Other institutional proposals will be made for the Community in the next few years. The outstanding question is whether the co-operation procedure, along with qualified majority voting, should be extended beyond matters affecting the internal market. But the essential matter is that relating to the Parliament. A proper solution could define the European role in national life more than anything else. There is no alternative to seeking greater standing for the Parliament. We should recall a phrase of Karl Popper's: 'Institutions are like fortresses. They must be well designed and manned.'

These fanciful suggestions are put forward neither to irritate, nor to amuse, but to remind the reader that the nation state, as it has grown in the shadow of Britain, France and Spain, has probably reached its term. The world wars were the logical conclusion of the process of nation-building which began in the sixteenth century. There was in Europe in 1914 an international upper class; an international trade union movement; and an international class of businessmen. Wars between states were in the interest of none of these. Those interests turned out to count for nothing. Chaos followed. It must be a background aim of Europe's new builders to seek to create not only a Europe where the risk of war between its nation states is removed – that seems certain – but one where the centralising thrust of the nation state is not repeated at the European level.

VIII
European Defence

The NATO communiqué in July 1990 included a remarkable innovation. I refer not to its astonishing invitation to President Gorbachev to address the North Atlantic Council, but to its support for the idea of finding a 'European identity in the domain of security'. Apparently President Mitterrand was responsible for this insertion. The idea has admittedly been in the public domain (though unofficially) for a long time. But in 1990 it at last became, not just fashionable, but conventional too. Sir Leon Brittan has spoken of it. I have already spoken (in Chapter I) of the contribution of Lord Carrington to this discussion.

The problem is complex. One member country of the European Community, Ireland, is not a member of NATO. France and Spain, members of the Community, are only qualified members of NATO. Three members of NATO (Norway, Iceland and Turkey) are not members of the Community.

Recent ideas for the construction of a real European security pillar have, therefore, recalled an old, half-forgotten institution: the Western European Union (WEU). This was founded in 1948. It was a forerunner of NATO, in which organisation its military functions were subsumed. All the same, it was maintained. It was useful in 1954 at the time of the collapse of the plans for the European Defence Community, affording Sir Anthony Eden a last diplomatic success before he was sucked into the prime ministership and disaster. What purpose WEU has fulfilled since then has been hidden from most of us. Still, it has nine members, all members of both the European Community and NATO. It has a headquarters and a secretary-general. This body has, therefore, been seen as a possible forum for the discussion of European defence in future.

If that be so, the discutants will, of course, have to take into account the willingness of both the Soviet Union and the United States to preserve, perhaps even expand in some ways, the 35-nation Conference for Security and Co-operation in Europe (CSCE), as well as maintain NATO and the Warsaw Pact, even if the original *raison d'être* of the former has evaporated, and if the latter seems in ruins.

The main immediate purpose of all these last-named bodies now seems to be disarmament and security, in a general sense. But they also provide a way for both the Soviet Union and the United States to play a part in, and have standing in, the heartland of Europe, which for the moment seems inevitable. The 350,000 or more Soviet troops in Germany will not go back home quickly, because there is no place for them to go. *Realpolitik* suggests that they must be balanced by United States troops.

NATO has also an obvious, important short-term purpose. The cold war may be over. The short-range weapons pointing at East Europe seem most inappropriate. But that only means that 'totalitarian imperialism' is no more. The 'Soviet threat' might be succeeded by a traditional kind of Russian menace. The Soviet Union still has a great arsenal of weapons and, despite everything, seems to be continuing to make them. Soviet chemical weapons exist in large numbers. She has innumerable SS-26s, modern tanks and Akula class submarines. Someone will control these in the Soviet Union and, if unopposed, could be tempted at least to threaten to use them. The nuclear weapons believed to be scattered around Russia, including some in states of that union which are wanting to secede, are disturbing. The Soviet army might come to political power. Its external policy might not include, initially at least, the subversion or overthrow of the West. But its long-term policies in such circumstances can only be guessed at.

The CSCE could be useful in extending disarmament on a large scale among both alliances. The future of the Warsaw Pact, on the other hand, is non-existent.

But in the long run, Europe, however defined, and in whatever forum, must surely collaborate in order to be able at least to aspire to look after herself.

This seems to be important since we do not know what are the futures of either of the nations which we have come to describe as 'superpowers' (since 1944, when the word was coined by W.T.R. Fox in his book of that title). The decay of the Soviet Union is plain to see; the future of the United States is less obvious. It will no doubt always have to be a Middle East power. Yet the increasing preoccupation of the United States with the Pacific, and the possibilities of a United States–Mexican common market (as well as the existing United States–Canadian one) will probably have the effect of drawing North Americans back to look on the problems of their own continent as primary ones. An astute United States' analyst, Angelo Codevilla, recently remarked: 'this is the right time to transfer full responsibility for the defence of Europe to the Europeans. This means reducing our military presence in Europe to little more than liaison and emergency preparedness.' Almost every other serious United States' commentator has said the same.

To see NATO as something which might turn into a political institution with a role beyond disarmament, and beyond the need to consider the aftermath of the end of the cold war, may turn out to be to perpetuate an institution after its purpose has gone. NATO was founded, and has lived, to face a particular, now vanishing, threat; it cannot be the right forum for the long term.

The nature of European defence in future is thus unclear. All the same, some splendid ideas have been unexpectedly launched: an ex-chief of staff has proposed the abolition of the RAF; a Conservative ex-minister has suggested 'a massive switch of resources ... from defence to education'. The benefit of considering the whole question now is that we can, to some extent, plan without taking into account past dispositions. It would have been a different matter if a European army had been established, as planned in 1954, under the aegis of the proposed, and now rarely lamented, European Defence Community. Old weapons and methods of organising men may survive. But collaboration between the nations of Europe on a new basis can be devised now almost *tabula rasa*. Such work as has already been done in the framework of NATO (for example, in the Eurogroup and the Independent European Programme Group, which includes France), or in respect of the Franco-German brigades, constitutes a good beginning.

The nature of the collaboration needed will be determined by projection of the likely enemies and threats. The biggest may derive from terrorism, particularly terrorism based on the exploitation of the difficulties, real or imagined, of minorities already within Europe. Countries of Africa or the Middle East are obviously likely to gain control of nuclear weapons and their method of delivery. So may terrorists. Quite a number, not just Iraq, are seeking ballistic missiles. Iraq has used chemical weapons against its own Kurdish citizens. (The neglect of the civilised countries to protest more violently was one of their greatest mistakes.) It has already spoken of using them in the Persian Gulf. Other nations may develop them too. Terrorists may gain access to them also.

Nearly 25 years after Harold Wilson demanded that Europe

act as one in critical matters in international affairs, European nations are still, as a rule, unable to act in common in defence of their interests. There may be a requirement for the policing of certain European frontiers, such as the Hungarian–Romanian one. European contingents may be required in United Nations' activities. These military functions may blend into semi-police usages. The Foreign Secretary has said that a European FBI might one day be a possibility: a 'Europolice' for the pursuit of drug traffickers as well as terrorists and even defrauders. 'British military doctrine' – a phrase inserted into the parlance of all senior officers of the British army, rather shyly, in 1989 – now specifies that 'the prime responsibility of the Government . . . to maintain the freedom and integrity of the United Kingdom . . . depends above all on peace in Europe'.

It would be wise to leave for later detailed discussion such questions as whether European defence in future should, in any real sense, include once more the formation of an army; and, if so, how the European character of it should be assured. There should not be any long political wrangling over the definition of, for example, 'the smallest possible unit', which caused such a controversy in the 1950s. No one wants a new European army which would be open to Churchill's famous (if in the circumstances of his previous advocacy, paradoxical) denunciation (see Chapter II). All that is now desirable is to indicate assumptions for a European defence – of which the first must be that the Europeans, by reason of their wealth and their capacity, ought to be able to imagine a future in which they themselves are, collectively, mainly responsible for their own defence; and secondly, that they should contemplate a time when the United States' presence in Europe has been either substantially reduced, or become non-existent.

If WEU is selected as the forum for organising common defence, it would have one obvious consequence – and, at least for the time being, benefit: namely, that that common defence would be formally and legally unconnected with the European Community itself. This would be helpful as a means of reassuring those who fear that the latter might be turning itself into a conventional superstate. On the other hand, even this association, under WEU's auspices, would be more than an alliance, since it would presumably be conceived of as permanent.

The idea of a 'European identity in the field of defence' may supply the key to the future of integration in the Community: not for what it does, but for what it does not do. There can be a European Parliament, a European political union, as well as a European agriculture, even a European currency (see Chapter IX); but while European nation states associate their military forces, as states, through the Western European Union (for example), rather then merge them, in some kind of body under the Community, they can still consider themselves independent in military matters. Even in an age of peace, the Brigade of Guards may still have an essential and, in this sense, tranquillising role. The disadvantage of this idea is that, as General Sir David Fraser has argued, defence, except in war itself, becomes deeply engaged in industry and the economy; the continued existence of independent national defence systems would cause unacceptable commercial rivalry. However, even if only a halfway stage, WEU may play a real part for, say, 25 years.

IX

European Money

The next issue is that of economic and monetary union. Doubtless I should have mentioned it earlier. But I place it last among the major issues in order to underline the fact that money, however sought after, merely points the way to ensure that society works properly. It is not, or should not be seen as, an end in itself, as those who make it soon realise.

The main item on the agenda of the European conference on this matter is, of course, the report of the committee of experts presided over by Jacques Delors. This was commissioned by the meeting of the European Council – that is, the heads of government – in June 1988 at Hanover: a venue which should have reminded the British participants of a continental connection in their country's golden age.

Jacques Delors and his collaborators proposed, in a document of 66 paragraphs (published in April 1989), the establishment, in three stages, of a European currency and the establishment of a European central bank (probably in Amsterdam or Luxembourg, not London nor Frankfurt). There would before that have been Europe-wide convergence of monetary policies. The committee of experts which produced the report had included all the governors of the European central banks (including the British).

The British Government's attitude to this report, as to the whole matter of European monetary union, has changed from time to time. It has seemed, indeed, a little 'Balfourian', as it used to be said, in the sense of giving the impression of walking on a tight-rope. But the Government's freedom of action on this matter is more limited than has sometimes been assumed. Though Britain refused in 1979 to join the Exchange Rate Mechanism (ERM) of the European Monetary System (EMS), and continued to refuse to do so throughout the 1980s, the Single European Act, which all member states ratified in 1987, says that all the governments 'approved the objective of the progressive realisation of Economic and Monetary Union'. This presumably is a treaty obligation, so that there should be no debate as to whether we shall join an EMU; only when. Further, the Government did accept, at the meeting of the European Council at Madrid, in 1989, the proposed first stage of the Delors Plan, to begin on 1 July 1990. That meant the completion of the internal market, the abolition of exchange controls, and membership of the ERM for all member states of the Community.

The first two things were easy enough for Britain: she had advocated the first and helped to initiate it; and she had abolished exchange controls in 1979. But the last of the three proposals was more difficult. Still, Britain accepted to join, in principle. That was, therefore, a decisive change. As John Major put it in September 1990, 'we have crossed the Rubicon'. (He took the plunge *into* the Rubicon in October – an event which *La Repubblica* in Italy kindly described as 'una bella giornata' for Europe.)

The second stage of Delors' scheme involves the preparation of new institutions, principally a European system of central banks. The third stage would involve the locking together of exchange rates and a move towards a single currency, the establishment of a European Central Bank, and a single monetary policy – including, in Delors' suggestion, limits on budgetary deficits. There would be comparable interest rates, a complete abolition of exchange controls, and general convergence of economic performance.

The tripartite element in the report may appear to link Delors with every good fairy story: the first stage is lead, the second silver, the third gold. But there is a difference: the commitment to lead is intended to imply an agreement to seek gold in the end. For there was an important sentence in the Delors report, stipulating that agreement to the first stage of the plan implied a commitment to continue to the end of 'the entire process'.

Nigel Lawson (Chancellor of the Exchequer until November 1989), who had become an advocate of British membership of the ERM, proposed, at a meeting in Antibes, in order to counter the second and third stages of the Delors plan, a scheme which would have allowed all European currencies to compete. It gained little backing. Lawson's British critics, such as Lord Cockfield, argued that adoption of that plan would mean that the leading currency of Europe would become the European currency: that is, the Deutschmark. Nigel Lawson left office. His plan lapsed.

Next, on 20 June, 1990, the new Chancellor of the Exchequer, John Major, introduced his much more ambitious and politically subtle scheme for a parallel currency, 'the hard ecu'. This new ecu would be guaranteed by a 'European monetary fund', which would be a committee of central bankers. That plainly might turn out to be a Bank of Europe in embryo. This hard ecu could also (so the Chancellor allowed) evolve into a European currency one day: ('in the very long term', he said in the last paragraph of his declaration launching the idea). His currency was named a 'hard' ecu, of course, to distinguish it from the existing ecu, which is the EMS's basket currency. It would be hard since it would be based on the Community's strongest currency, not on the average one – as is the case with the existing ecu. Expressing his thanks, in an unusual act of official generosity to Sir Michael Butler, a recently retired ambassador to the Community, John Major made an excellent case for his idea in so far as it would assist travellers and small traders. The Governor of the Bank of England, who had signed the Delors report with his fellow-governors of central banks, argued in favour of this plan on the tactical ground that movement to a single currency quickly might cause 'intolerable strains' by, for example, insisting on the early standardisation of interest rates.

John Major's plan had the political advantage that it could be presented to the continental Europeans as a provisional proposal; and, to the British, as something which might last a long time: *rien ne dure que le provisoire*, the House of Commons could be assured. In John Major's scheme, inflation would be prevented by arranging that central banks which devalued would make up the value of the EMF's holding of their currency to the same amount of ecus. They would use their reserves to do this.

It seemed, to begin with, that John Major's proposal (which, he said, was 'put forward for discussion') had been introduced too late to influence the other Europeans, who had mostly become attracted by the idea of moving quickly to a single currency – both for itself and because of its obvious part in preparing the way to a political union. Jacques Delors talked in early 1990 of hoping to move ahead to begin the second stage of economic and monetary union on 1 January 1993. But several countries then began to question the speed of Delors' plan. Would not early adoption of Stage II cause 'maladjustments'? And inflation? And, perhaps, lead to expensive and ineffective regional policies? At the same time, the Italian Government said that 'the Major proposals have some interesting points, like the idea of enhancing the importance of the ecu during Stage II of the Delors plan'. At the meeting of European ministers of finance in September 1990, Carlos Solchaga, the Spanish Minister, actually backed John Major. So, with reservations, did his German colleague – not so much because he liked the idea of the hard ecu, but because he did not like Delors' proposed speed which, he thought, might undermine German monetary stability.

This means a very considerable success for John Major. It remains nevertheless true that, over the eleven years since 1979, the continental European currencies have become slowly locked together around the Deutschmark. The Benelux countries are already fully in the zone of the Mark. They, and France, still want to go ahead to full monetary union now, including a single currency, principally because they see it as the only effective way of giving them control, or at least a hand in the control, of their economic fate: the alternative to dominance by the Deutschmark. A European currency, with a 'EuroFed', would give countries other than Germany at least a voice in the management of the European currency.

The reaction of these countries to John Major's plan is still that it is not necessary: if a single currency is the aim, why not go straight for it by, for example, narrowing the bands of the exchange rate mechanism, progressively fixing rates, and then instituting a currency reform? Partly too, the French fear that the present opportunity may not recur. Every educated Frenchman knows the saying of Cardinal de Retz: *'Il n'y a rien dans le monde qui n'ait son moment decisif; et le chef d'oeuvre de la bonne conduite est de le reconnaître et de prendre ce moment.'* In consequence, France has already minted a coin which is denominated on one side in francs, on the other in ecus. The Belgians have minted ecus which have been accepted in taxis, hotels and restaurants in Brussels.

Early in 1990 the German Government and Karl Otto Pöhl seemed prepared to make the 'enormous sacrifice of sovereignty', as the latter put it to the Select Committee on Economic and Monetary Union of the House of Lords on 3 July 1990, of abandoning the Deutschmark for a European currency, for two reasons: because they hoped that thereby the European

Community would help them to bail out East Europe, including East Germany; and because, at least for the moment, they found the idea of European federalism in the monetary field acceptable. But in the middle of the year, with unification almost a reality, and preoccupied by the political threat to monetary stability posed by East German poverty, their enthusiasm for Jacques Delors' timetable waned.

No doubt, Britain will seek an understanding on monetary union with Germany. British diplomats will insist that the hard ecu could be the free marketeers' suggestion for a European currency, much more suitable for freedom-loving German bankers than the 'euro-currency' of Delors. Germans, like the British, are attached to their existing currency. Yet the consequences of this diplomacy, if successful, might not all be to our long-term advantage. We might save our faces. But do we prefer the Deutschmark to be the *de facto* European currency, with the British pound sterling nominally, yet only nominally, independent – in fact, even more reliant on the Deutschmark than it is now? Where, anyway, would the strong ecu go in such circumstances?

The conference which opened in December 1990 on monetary union may decide (some time in the summer of 1991) in favour of creating a central bank for Europe, with ultimately a common currency. Britain may then have to choose between accepting that, and so remain within the 'inner circle'; and refusing, and, therefore, withdraw from it. With London aspiring to be the financial capital of a united Europe, we must surely, however reluctantly, choose to remain inside. The consequence of remaining in this matter 'the last ship in the convoy', would be bad for British hopes of encouraging investment, bad for the City of London (as a financial centre) and would prevent our playing any part in the future shaping of the Community. In this respect the authors of a recent pamphlet issued by the Institute for Public Policy Research are surely right: they 'conclude that, while a gradualist approach may be optimal, and should be supported in negotiation, it may not prove attainable. If it does not, the United Kingdom should accept the majority EC view, since the alternative of standing aside from the whole process would be far worse.'

In practice, however, John Major's proposals might turn out to be closer to, or more adaptable to, those of a majority of Community members than they seem at first sight. That 'European monetary fund' of his could be strengthened, surely, as the Germans have suggested, to turn into a bank. John Major's European currency 'in the very long term' might turn out to be sooner than it sounds. It often does in politics; everyone remembers how long Harold Wilson believed a week to be. Señor Solchaga would not expect the Eurocurrency to be with us before AD 2000. Perhaps that could be seen as 'a very long term'. The appeal of the hard ecu might also be considerable. Gresham's Law provided the theory that bad money drives out good. But that was in the age of bimetallism, not of two currencies, such as the pound and the ecu. Any plan, meantime, for joining a monetary union, while arranging to seek a special position to enable the pound to be continued to be used indefinitely for domestic purposes, would repeat the mistake of 1979.

If pressed to choose between supporting independence for the Central Bank instead of 'accountability', Britain should of course choose the first, since the latter word is a synonym for political control. Such 'control' would be at the mercy of national elections, of which there might be an average of two a year in the Community of twelve.

The purpose of the new Central Bank, if formed, would obviously be to preserve the stability of prices, as the Bundesbank is formally asked to do. The governors of the Bank should be named to ensure that. Herr Pöhl was right to insist to the Select Committee in the House of Lords that stability of prices was an inherent good. The reverse is equally true. Other roles which central bankers this century have, in national circumstances, sometimes assumed – that of assisting governments to ensure full employment, or to carry out, by fiscal policy, various social aspirations – would be to 'trespass on the terrain of Member States', as the European Commissioner for Competition, Sir Leon Brittan, skilfully put it. (John Major's European monetary fund would, presumably, also be insulated from politics, as from the pursuit of popularity.)

The Financial Times, in a leader on 11 September 1990, suggested that, as well as agreeing to a strengthening of John Major's monetary fund to become something like the Bank envisaged by others, the British Government could gain even more backing for its hard ecu by saying positively that, in the end, it saw that becoming the Community's currency. That idea is an intelligent one. The Government, in its attachment to old methods of managing money, may underestimate the attractions, for the electorate of the future, of a European currency. A new currency which holds its value could turn out to have many attractions over an old one, even the pound sterling, which does not. 'Sterling in danger', Sir Alan Walters trumpets, vaguely recalling an old cartoon of Gillray's, 'Political Ravishment, or The Old Lady of Threadneedle Street in Danger'. But it may be that the nation has come to prefer predictability to patriotic memory. The cost of maintaining twelve separate currencies in a single customs union has already come to seem to many people, particularly small traders and individual travellers, to be high. Few people, even on the Left, I suspect, would be sorry to say goodbye to the financial management of 1945–79, whereby government after government sought to escape from a crisis over the balance of payments by devaluation or by inflationary wage settlements. A free trading area is manageable, with floating exchange rates between individual currencies. But it has been shown to be unsatisfactory. Such rates have not prevented major swings of value and unpredictable misalignments. A common market without a common currency, as Sir Leon Brittan has said, may also turn out to seem an anachronism. The only people who would gain by such a thing would be speculators in currencies, money-changers and banks (whose profits from having many currencies to change has been calculated on the Continent as being as much as 1.5 per cent of national income – and whose reaction to the prospect of abolishing fees for changing money has already been seen as explosive).

The effect on inflation of a single currency is, certainly, debatable. The experience of the EMS suggests, however, that it would be positive, for the EMS has, *pace* Sir Alan Walters, been a success in recent years. It has given stability to exchange rates and seems to have assisted a convergence of inflation. The inner five countries of the 'Schengen group' have achieved low inflation, varying from 2.2 per cent in the Netherlands to 3 per cent in Belgium. Those five countries are also convinced that a common currency will afford lower rates of interest. Equally, alignments of currencies have been few. Obviously an increase in internal European trade would be likely. Therefore, we should contemplate a world in which the ecu may become our measure of wealth and, in the long run, the main one.

European monetary union has been opposed by many people, including some ministers, on the ground that an agreement to have it would constitute abandonment of national independence. The right to print a national currency, and the capacity to change interest rates, are seen as the prime indicators of sovereign power. Yet this may be more a matter of appearance than of reality. Much has been made of the decision to raise British base rates of money half an hour after the German decision. Yet there really is no answer to the argument implicit in pointing the moral in that. Leon Brittan has recalled that, throughout the golden age of stability between 1815 and 1914, there was 'a single international currency: sterling, dollars, marks and francs were simply the local names of gold'. Those who complain about the use of the ecu, a

French name even if it does mean European Currency Unit, might be soothed by recalling that l.s.d. stood for *librae*, *solidi*, and *denarii*, all Roman coins introduced into England by Lombard bankers. It is questionable whether the control of money, in the twenty-first century, will seem the badge of nationhood. Economists will disagree with this scepticism because they have personally benefited from an era when they have been extensively used by governments for a manipulation of the supply of money. But, 'the standpoint from which to comprehend the economic history of great cultures is not to be looked for on economic grounds', correctly wrote Spengler. Already we are close to, or at least are familiar with, an international currency: namely, the dollar. Tables of statistics, which we consult, are usually in dollars and are perfectly understood. No one's hackles rose, patriotically at least, when it was revealed that the Soviet miners gave $1-million to their British comrades at the time of the miners' strike of 1984. Nor do commentators refuse to discuss the price of oil in dollars. In the next twelve months, I expect to give lectures in four separate countries. None of them is the United States. Yet my fees will be paid in dollars. There are better indices of national character.

The decision, at Rome, of the European Council to try to begin Stage II of the Delors plan on 1 January 1994 upset the British. But the decision is bound to have the beneficial effect of forcing Britain to consider what they really expect from the European Monetary Union to which they are committed. Perhaps a postponement could be assured if the Government were to accept John Major's 'in the very long run', for the transformation of his hard ecu into a European currency, could be the year 2000.

X

The Community and the Rest of Europe

The events of the age of *glasnost* and *perestroika* in Russia cast shadows over all Europe, west as well as east. We have observed not just the defeat of communism, but a transformation of Russia: 'Where once the Russian flag has flown, it must not be lowered again', was Tsar Nicholas I's order in 1850, in respect of Nevelskoy's settlement at the mouth of the river Amur. But that Tsarist instruction has been gone back upon, as well as many others of the age of 'totalitarian imperialism'. Gorbachev's friend and spokesman, Georgi Arbatov, has told an audience of Cuban exiles in Miami that the Soviet Government now regrets the almost 90-billion roubles which it made available to the third world: 'the occasional petty victories' on the 'cold war' battlefield of the third world were meaningless in comparison with the 'tremendous damage' caused to world peace.

The frame within which the European Community lives is affected by the fact that one of the drives behind it at the beginning, the need for small states to come together in the face of the Russian juggernaut (as they had not done in the 1930s in the face of the Nazis), exists no longer. Events are also affected by the realisation that, partly in consequence of the success of Western Europe, political as well as economic, the peoples of communist Europe are returning to something like the place which they held before the tragedy of the second world war. The people of East Germany are once again fully Germans and, hence, nationals of the Community. If the East Germans have obtained that, it will be difficult indefinitely to exclude Poles, Czechs, and Hungarians. Nor should we want to. Those who live in Cracow are at least as European, by any definition of the word, as those who live in Brighton – as Mrs Thatcher very correctly indicated in her famous speech at Bruges long before the collapse of those communist regimes. Before that, in 1984, Milan Kundera had pointed out that the plight of old central Europe was 'a drama of the West – a West that, kidnapped, displaced, and brainwashed, nevertheless insists on defending its identity'. He added: 'the word "Europe" does not represent a phenomenon of geography but a spiritual notion synonymous with the West.' (Until recently we had the habit of calling these countries 'Eastern Europe'. Before 1939 we called them 'Central Europe', *Mitteleuropa*. We should, as Dr Brzezinzki insisted in 1988, call them that again, and use the alternative terminology for states which are eastward-*facing*.) Beyond those states there are 'the Balkans': Yugoslavia, Albania, Romania and Bulgaria. However unsatisfactory we, at the moment, perceive some of those countries' progress towards democracy, they cannot be left on one side. They too belong to 'the drama of the West'.

It must be one of the main tasks of Western Europe to assist all these nations back towards the civil, or civilised, life to which they subscribed, to a varying extent, before 1939. France and Britain agree on this; it was a theme of Mrs Thatcher's speech at Aspen, Colorado, in 1990; it explains President Mitterrand's proposal on 1 January 1990 for confederation. Here, as in respect of monetary union, France sees the Community as the best way to harness Germany. Some of these nations of *Mitteleuropa* have (or had), of course, great traditions – not purely artistic and literary, though these are important. But Hungary and Poland at the end of the eighteenth century had a long history of parliamentary government, even if the parliamentarians were of one class – the gentry in both cases, with Latin the official language in Hungary until 1848. Bohemia, though not 'Czechoslovakia', was a mediaeval monarchy. All the countries concerned have had some experience of elections, a free market, political parties and an independent judiciary – even if incompletely.

The establishment of a European Bank for Reconstruction and Development in London, under the direction of Jacques Attali, will turn out to be only the first of much necessary institutional assistance to these countries. Environmental help will be another, as every day new stories come out of the ex-communist states: 55 per cent of East Germany's forests damaged; 70 per cent of Czechoslovakia's. Bronislaw Kaminski, the Polish Minister for the Environment, said, at the first meeting which he and other Eastern European holders of environmental portfolios had with western colleagues, that the Silesian industrial area was 'the most polluted part of Europe'. The European Environmental Agency will have much to do. Then there is the question of Eastern European agriculture. The needs of the European Community for food could be almost satisfied if West Europeans were able to buy more easily the product of the East's great plains. But to arrange this would involve a commitment to reform the CAP in a radical manner.

There is also the likelihood that if there is a common (Western) European currency, it would soon become the usual currency of most of the ex-communist states. The Deutschmark is, after all, already in general use in Central Europe.

Lurking behind these questions is the uncomfortable realisation that, first, these states are sovereign ones with now no commonly accepted international linkage; second, that they are all likely to be unceremoniously linked together by their Western friends as either *Mitteleuropa* or areas with 'traditional' ties to Germany.

We should not expect recovery soon; the destruction caused by, first, conquest by Germany and then 'liberation' and communisation by Russia, may take two generations to overcome. We should avoid deductions drawn from history. Bohemia was the industrial heart of the later Habsburg Empire. But the 'advanced' character of that economy was partly due either to the Jews or to the Germans – both of whom were destroyed between 1938 and 1947. Comparable considerations are relevant to most of the countries concerned. None of the countries concerned is an old nation state with a continuous history; in one sense, Czechoslovakia and Poland, despite their antiquity, are graduates of the class of 1919, as is Yugoslavia; Romania and Bulgaria are of the class of 1878; and Hungary is of that of 1867. The Treaty of Saint Germain, leading to the break-up of Austria-Hungary, was as unfair as that of Versailles. Some of the lines then established are bound to be reconsidered. The ideas for a federation between Poland and Czechoslovakia put by General Sikorski to Dr Beneš in 1940 could also be re-examined. If there were no Czechoslovak federation with Poland (at the very thought of which Czechs hold up their hands in astonishment!), Slovakia could separate from Bohemia. The integrity of Yugoslavia may not survive. The clash between territorial and linguistic nationalism which first inspired, and then destroyed, Central Europe between 1848 and 1945, could revive.

It has been argued, reasonably, that the revival of liberty in these states in Central Europe should cause Western Europe to delay further movements towards integration. But the majority of the members of the Community think that they should, on the contrary, go ahead as fast as possible, 'deepening' before 'enlarging', so as to be able to make possible a united approach to East and Central Europe, to avoid a risk of chaos and instability.

The Foreign Ministers of the twelve member states of the Community echoed those views when they insisted that we should carry through the arrangements upon which we have embarked in Western Europe before associating other countries, however deserving candidates the countries may be. That is, the Single Market must be finished; whatever is decided on in respect of monetary union must be in effect; and whatever elements of political union are desired will have been embarked upon.

Thus no new candidate for membership will be considered until 1993. Then the first candidates to be allowed to present themselves will be Austria and Turkey. There is unfairness in this, because of the favoured treatment which the former East Germans will be achieving. East Germany may have been the strongest of the communist countries before 1989, but it was one of the worst. Its character was expressed by the brutality of the *Volkspolizei* at the Berlin Wall and by its ecological outrages. Still, for a nation which has been divided for 45 years and, essentially, occupied by communists as well, good luck should not be grudged. All the same, if East Germans have become 'European Community nationals', Austria will not be easily rejected. If Austria is in, Hungary will have to be considered. And then there is Poland, which has not only its Silesian Germans talking of 'a Europe without borders', but its special moral position as having been those who 'set the dogs to spring the game which, as soon as they had done, was seized by others' (an image used about the role of Portugal in the European discoveries of the sixteenth century). What then of Czechoslovakia whose plight between 1948 and 1989 was largely due to their abandonment in 1938 by France and Britain? Romania and Bulgaria's connections with Western civilisation go back to antiquity.

The reason for excluding all but East Germany for the moment is that the application by four new countries from EFTA (Austria, Switzerland, Norway and Sweden), and perhaps of as many as seven from the wrecks of communism (Poland, Czechoslovakia, Hungary, Romania, Yugoslavia, Bulgaria and Albania) would pose a challenge of the greatest difficulty. The Community of twelve works quite well. One of 23 would imply a different undertaking. There would be a serious possibility of its breaking up. There would also, contrariwise, be a drive towards greater central authority in order to enable decisions to be taken at least as easily as they are today.

Several of the countries of EFTA and the ex-communist countries may, in the end, not wish to become full members of the Community. They could settle for that abysmally named compromise, the European Economic Space (EES), which may enable some member states to participate in the Single Market without subscribing to the constraints of the Community. All the same, EES will probably turn out, like EFTA itself, to be no more than a waiting-room, 'a transit station' for those who would like eventually to set off on the journey to full membership. The countries of EFTA have already abolished tariffs with the Community. This has led to substantial trade: the latter's exports to the six countries of EFTA are as big as those to the United States and Japan combined. But the closer and stricter Community regulations (for example, on subsidies and dumping) are causing many new problems to both sides.

Nor is the list of possible candidates exhausted at the mention of these names. Beyond the Balkans, Turkey is a serious candidate – and one to whom, in the past, for strategic rather than economic reasons, encouragement has been given. There are also nations of the Soviet Union which may, one day, want some kind of association with the Community: the Baltic states, for example, and both Armenia and Georgia. All three Baltic states were, in the 1980s, for example, embraced by Radio Free Europe (which broadcast to communist Europe) instead of, as until then, Radio Liberty (which broadcast to Russia). If Poland is a part of Europe, it seems unhistorical to exclude Lithuania. The two countries have heroes in common (Adam Mickievicus, or Adam Mickiewitz), as well as many common problems (the status of Vilnius). Ukraine, Latvia and Estonia have similar relations, and comparable difficulties.

Whatever arrangements can be made to help these nations, a core is necessary for Europe. Only once it is firmly established will it be possible to contemplate new arrangements.* This will be dismissed by some as 'a French view', but the case for it is strong.

In the meantime, the process of assistance to the ex-communist countries must continue. The fact that, at the Western economic summit of 1989, the United States (like Japan) agreed that their aid to these countries should be organised through Brussels is a major factor.

Statesmanship will, of course, be required to ensure that Western Europe has time to fulfil its own plans but, at the same time, avoid disappointment, and hence resentment, among the countries whose needs are pressing. The euphoria at the end of communism in those countries is already dying down. Peoples and governments are observing that the 45 years of communism constituted a kind of plaster of paris which did not heal the broken limbs of the nations concerned; they acted as a concealment. The continuing crisis in the Soviet Union will affect matters. How would Poland (in association with Europe) look on a newly independent Ukraine?

The era before the first world war and the communist revolutions seems golden in retrospect. It had glories. All the same, that age's greatest writer, Henry James, referred to the 1890s as marked by 'the madness, the passions, the hideous clumsiness of rage'. Communism was a solution to these and other evils put forward by highly motivated men and women (many of them admirably brave in appalling circumstances), to

*See the speech of the Foreign Secretary, 11 June 1990, quoted in *The Financial Times* 12 June 1990, where he says the applications of Austria and Turkey will not be considered until 1993.

correct some of those evils. The solution failed in practice, but new ideas will be necessary. In Russia, as in the whole of Europe, we are seeing momentous and complicated intellectual and moral processes, the effects and consequences of which cannot be foreseen. Western Europe is a participant, as well as an observer, in a process which is bound to end, surely, with *Mitteleuropa* and the Balkans eventually joining the Community – even if this does not happen before 2025.

I have deliberately avoided discussion here of President Gorbachev's insistence that the Soviet Union is part of the 'common European home' (or 'house'). In a sense, that is true: Moscow often seems to be a city of *Mitteleuropa*; Russian culture, particularly Russian literature, is part of the European heritage. Russia has been a European power since the reign of Peter the Great. But the reality is that Russia cannot expect, neither as Russia alone nor as the Soviet Union, to be part of the European Union of the future, any more than the United States can. The disproportion would be too great. President Gorbachev realises this. The 'common home' is becoming a largely cultural idea, having been at first a propaganda one. Yet these sensible comments may turn out to be vain if the Soviet Union were to collapse into civil war. The European Community would not be tempted, presumably, into intervention in the style of what happened in 1918–21. All the same, the existence of Germans, Jews and Armenians in the Soviet multi-national state might, however tragically, persuade us that the 'European house' stretched at least as far as Yerevan; or, perhaps that Europe had a 'Russian home'.

XI

And the Consequences are . . .

The British have a tendency to suppose that they alone among the nations of Europe have deep ties of blood and common culture with ex-imperial countries colonised by us in the past, whether with the Commonwealth or with the United States. But France, Portugal and Spain are other European countries which have emotional tugs towards ex-empires. A Mexican president returns to an ancient home in Spain which his ancestors left for 'America' several hundred years ago, just as a North American one might to, say, Leicester or County Down. Ireland, in many ways, despite its majestic parochiality, is the least 'European' country of the Community. But it has at least as close relations with the United States as Britain has.

These relations should not be ignored. Rather, they should be used as a springboard to ensure that these nations, including ourselves, lead the Community to take active steps, both before 1992 and after, to ensure that the great issue of the liberalisation of world trade is not forgotten while we are engaging in achieving the Single Market. (Margaret Thatcher spoke of this eloquently at Aspen in 1990.) David Henderson, the head of the Economics and Statistics department of the OECD, has recently pointed out that developing countries are now, for the first time, giving 'the main impetus for freer trade'; while only four of the twenty-four advanced industrial countries – Turkey, Japan, Australia and New Zealand – can claim to be more liberal than they were in 1980. None of them is European.

Of course, there will be unexpected consequences for Britain if she seriously makes the choice to remain in the thick of European development, rather than one of the other two choices named in Chapter IV – which would distance her from it. There would be changes throughout our politics. For example, an increase in the power of the European Parliament, or a change in its functions, would affect the House of Commons, even if an effort is made simultaneously to achieve more effective relations between the Council of Ministers and national parliaments; and the House of Commons is the most famous legislative assembly in the Community, with an uninterrupted history of centuries, which makes all others seem to be merely created yesterday.

But all institutions, if they are to survive, must evolve. 'There is no growth without change', wrote Cardinal Newman. The House of Commons is a wonderfully lively place. It is still one of the few legislatures in the world where speeches are made, not read out. Debates there are real. All the same, the growth of party, and of party whipping, has made the Commons a less effective check on executive power than it used to be in, say, the eighteenth and nineteenth centuries. Men and women seek to become members of the House of Commons to try and climb the greasy pole to ministerial office – unlike those who enter the House of Representatives in the United States. The twice-weekly clash between the Prime Minister and the Leader of the Opposition is, as a regular thing, very modern: Its 'gladiatorial' character pleases the performers, and now the television producers, but, by emphasising division, creates party conflict even in respect of matters where none exists.

Television has also already changed politics a good deal – for the worse, as I believe: consider the eclipse of the political meeting and the bizarre 'standing ovations' at the end of party conferences. (The castration of the House of Lords by the Parliament Act of 1911 was a setback too; instead of cutting the powers of the upper House, its composition should have been altered).

There will also be some consequences for the Crown. There is no question of the monarchy losing its place, nor of its assuming the humble place before superior power which was the fate of German kings after the foundation of the German empire in 1870. But if certain elements of power are transferred by a new Treaty of Subsidiarity and, even more, if there are regular meetings of heads of state, even of an informal nature, something will have undoubtedly changed. Symbolically this will seem important. But then, already, the Queen in Parliament has had to receive Community legislation as directives; and Community regulations do not even have to go to the Queen and the legislature, though consequential legislation may be necessary.

So I return to the need for that deep breath which I mentioned earlier as being necessary: we need to start trying to do what the French and all the others have done, and identify the national interest with that of the Community. 'Much of the opposition to the Community in Britain turns out to be at bottom a largely sub-conscious nostalgia', a British General wrote to me recently; 'it is one of the strongest forces in politics both Left and Right.' The arguments deployed by those who dislike what I have argued here, are often rationalisations which merely prove that.

The choice before us is frankly not black. No other once great nation which has been the centre of an empire has had, after that empire's eclipse, the chance of entering immediately into so potentially powerful a union as the European Community. Recall the fate of Spain, France, the Ottoman Empire, Austria–Hungary. Civil war engulfed them, as it may engulf Russia.

Having voluntarily absented ourselves in the 1950s from its creation, we did not help to shape the new Europe. Had we been intimately engaged from 1950 onwards as a participating member state, *Europe à l'anglaise* (whatever that was) could have been achieved. But despite what we think of as the Community's continental eccentricities, it is still a structure with which we should be able to live. 'Free marketeers' should think big enough to embrace the whole of Europe. Equally, Tory 'Wets' and the Socialists alike must recognise that paternalism in one country will not work: the nation state is just too small a frame for the twenty-first century. This should be easier than it seems: the basic ideas behind all these approaches – capitalism, aristocracy and socialism – were all, for many generations, international ones. It was the newly-educated petty bourgeoisie of the nineteenth century which, after the French Revolution, caused the nation state to assume its familiar shape.

Many British subjects could find – have already found – membership of a united Europe an inspiration. To carry out in peace and liberty, with a Continent-wide market, with real devolution of powers, what Philip II, Louis XIV, Napoleon, the Kaiser and Hitler sought to achieve by force is a noble task – not a visitation to be endured. The CAP is still bad, but it is also still reformable. There are other things which we judge ridiculous. They too can be improved, even suppressed. Only a lack of vigilance or intelligence (on our part) could allow the Community to turn into a centralised state of the kind run by *énarques* which many fear. We should, in short, recall the spirit of Winston Churchill (no peroration to a political essay in the twentieth century is complete without him) – but the young, clear-headed, Liberal statesman of the 1910s, not the contradictory one of the late 1940s – when he remarked:

> 'The changes that are to come
> I do not fear to see.'

When we visit a country outside Europe, and we see the trade of that country measured not in terms of volume exchanged with Britain, France, etc., but with the 'European Community', it is easy to fall into the habit of thinking that a European union already exists. Other peoples consider that we are already a fully enthusiastic member of the European club. For example, in 1990 I went to that strange spring festival, *las Fallas*, in Valencia. The winning exhibit depicted Europe's welcome to Spain. The scene shown was of a Don Juanesque cavalier being greeted on what looked like the Rialto bridge by a buxom odalisque. He was about to be led to see the great European sights. These included the Eiffel Tower, naturally, but also Big Ben.

Except during the climax of empire in the nineteenth century (when all European nations were empires), our history has always been part of continental history – just as our arts have been interwoven with those of the Continent. In the high days of empire, rivalry with other European empire-builders dominated our politics. Throughout the Middle Ages, England was a continental power; during much of that time, our laws were written in French. Over half of Shakespeare's plays are set on the Continent. Donizetti and Verdi certainly regarded English literature as part of their own heritage, as they made Scott and Shakespeare the excuses for operas. The Stuarts were all half-French, either in blood or disposition. From 1714 until 1837, our monarchs were electors or kings of Hanover, and, from the first of these two dates until 1952, it would have taxed the most agile genealogist to find a drop of English blood among our rulers. Our architecture is obviously a part of European architecture, just as our literature and music are of European art.

It is true that a precisely contrary point of view could be put in an isolationist history of England. Such a volume, however, would have to dwell on many things already lost: the old parochial Tory party of the eighteenth century, for example, at whose meetings at the Cocoa Tree in Pall Mall or the 'British Coffee House' in

Cockspur Street, brooches sold in the shape of warming pans. The liberty which those old Tories loved was, Sir Keith Feiling told us, 'a Conservative goddess, surrounded by independent squires'. Of course, our liberties are ancient, but often past electoral campaigns were like those of the Duke of Newcastle: 'long slow electoral tours in which he was rarely sober for days but the outcome was an outstanding success.' Anyone who truly appreciates the real charms of old England, the vigour of its old parliamentary life, its tolerance, its understated wit, and its greenwood (now scarcely visible, alas, because of progressive agriculture), knows that our history has been a part of European history, not just of the island which Michelet and, through him, de Gaulle, affected to observe through fog. 'We Europeans are children of Hellas', wrote H.A.L. Fisher, in the first lines of his *History of Europe*, a work which influenced my generation more than any other book of history; he added, 'the broad fact remains: there *is* an European Civilisation'. In blood, of course, most 'British' have common ancestors with all the other Celtic or Germanic peoples. England does not have the heritage of Roman law (though Scotland does). The Roman Church played only a subterranean part here for 200 years in 'early modern history'. All the same, England and Wales were for nearly 350 years a part of the Roman Empire. So we too can look back on the 'long Roman peace' which that colossal enterprise offered, as part of a then united structure, and seek, with the backward glance that has often marked effective innovators, to revive as well as to build.

Britain's relation to Europe has, over the last few years, a certain similarity with that of Tarquin and the Sibylline books. Tarquin, it will be recalled, was at first uninterested in the nine books offered at a high price by one of the Sibyls. She burned three books and offered Tarquin six of the books at the same price as the nine. He refused again. She burned three more books, and offered Tarquin the last three at the same high price as the nine and the six. This behaviour astonished Tarquin. He paid the asking price. So should we in order to remain within the European cavalcade.